A Series Of Seven Essays On Universal Science: Embracing Some Investigations Of The Mosaic Cosmogony, And The Interpretation Of The Scriptures, With The Object Of Proving Their Scientific Exactness

Thomas Clark Westfield

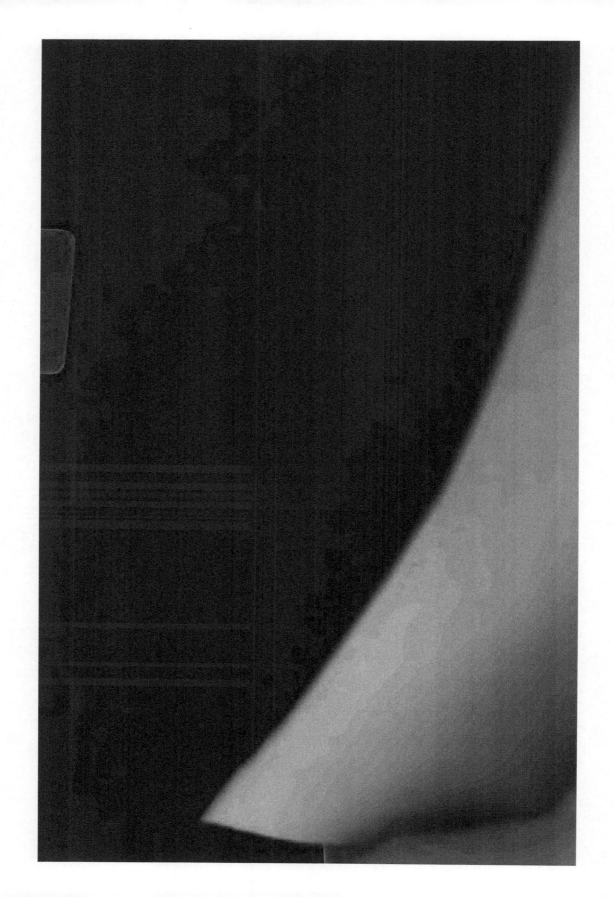

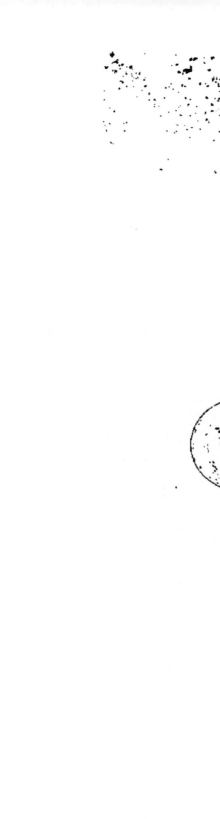

A SERIES

OF

SEVEN ESSAYS

ON

UNIVERSAL SCIENCE,

EMBRACING SOME

INVESTIGATIONS OF THE MOSAIC COSMOGONY, AND THE INTER-
PRETATION OF THE SCRIPTURES, WITH THE OBJECT OF
PROVING THEIR SCIENTIFIC EXACTNESS.

BY

THOMAS CLARK WESTFIELD, F.S.A.

LONDON:
ROBERT HARDWICKE, 192, PICCADILLY.
1863.

ENTERED AT STATIONERS' HALL.

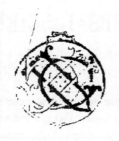

GEORGE UNWIN, PRINTER, BUCKLERSBURY, LONDON, E.C.

PREFACE.

Our chief object in bringing the following essays before the notice of the public has been to endeavour to investigate, in an intelligible and straightforward manner, the subjects upon which so much contention has been manifested; and also to endeavour to prove, not only the truth but the scientific exactness of the Scriptures. We believe, most assuredly, that there is not one fact stated in the whole Bible that is not scientifically correct, or may be accounted for, either by some slight error in translation, or our imperfect knowledge of the subject.— *God's works cannot contradict His words.*

We must crave the indulgence of our readers in submitting to them, in the course of

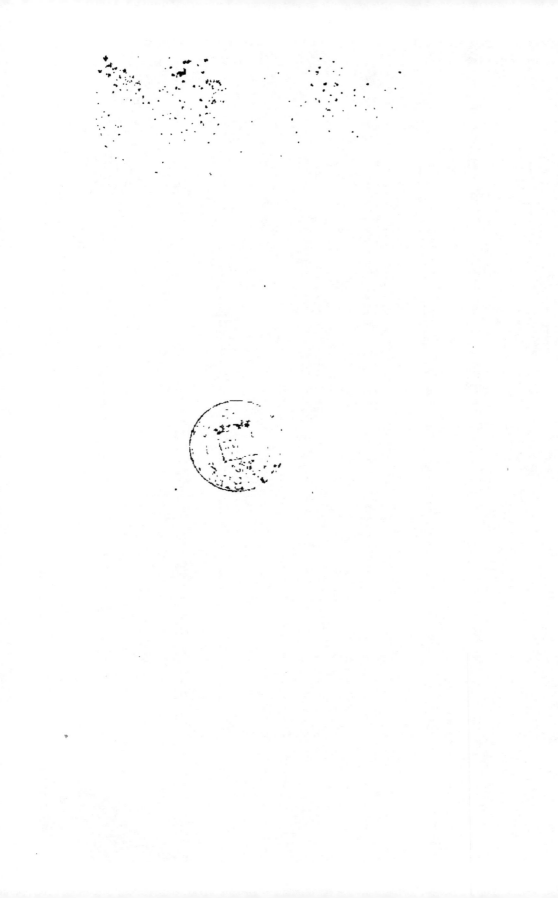

... Scripture;" and therefore dealt with the ... ... fullin ... accordingly, although his ... ... theorists have gone far to prove their scientific ... ... correctness, and certainly were never advanced ... ... in opposition to the Bible.

THOS. CLARK WESTFIEL...

Corpus Hall,
16th September, 1868.

CONTENTS.

ESSAY V.

ON MATTER AND ITS PROPERTIES.

ESSAY VI.

ON THE IMMENSITY OF THE UNIVERSE.

ESSAY VII.

ON THE MULTIPLICITY OF WORLDS.

INTRODUCTION.

THE study of science in connection with revelation and the expounding of Divine truth, is certainly the noblest and most absorbing occupation of the human mind ; and as it is the same beneficent Creator who formed the world and instituted the physical laws which are the foundation of all science, that also caused by the inspiration of His word the Scriptures to be written, we must expect to find that both, *being properly understood*, must agree even to the minutest particular ; any other supposition would do violence to human reason and understanding. Nevertheless, we find those who are constantly arming themselves with science to assault truth, as it is revealed to us in the Scripture. For this there must be some palpable cause or reason, and what is it ? To our minds this question is readily answered. First, from an incompetency to judge by an insufficient knowledge of the subject——which knowledge future revela-

b

tions and discoveries in science may supply—
or, what is less likely, misconceptions arising
from errors in translation.

We know that the inspiration of the Scriptures is looked upon in a great many different
lights, and while many admit of the inspiration of the truths concerning theology, the
gospel, and our salvation, allow themselves
to be deluded into the idea that errors may
make their appearance when the same writers,
under the same inspiration, are treating on
physical truths. God is equally the Author
of both ; and if we allow ourselves to believe
that errors occur on the one hand, we must
also admit of them on the other. In such a
case, the Bible would cease to be of the immense
importance it is, and would be reduced, for the
most part, to a simple historical account of the
Jews, and even that an imperfect one. But
recognising in every page of it the inspired
Word of God, we can admit of no error,
whether treating on physical truths or truths
concerning theology and religion. It is, indeed,
a melancholy fact that so many scientific men
have been sceptics, and wrongly applied the
interpretation of science; but this is by no
means a necessary result from its study. On the
contrary, its tendency has been proved in the
highest degree favourable to religious devotion,

and therefore some more potent cause must have influenced certain eminent scientific men to the adoption of views antagonistic to religion and piety.

We have repeatedly found that when men employ their scientific knowledge to the detriment and injury of the Scriptures, the knowledge possessed has neither been very deep or profound; in fact, the very limited knowledge which they possess causes a confusion and antagonism of their ideas which they imagine clash with religious truth, and without troubling themselves to study the subject more deeply, give publicity to their views, to the injury, often, of many simple and unscientific readers. Happily it ends there, for their works generally get into the hands of those who are able, from their deeper knowledge, to dissuade the public mind from their abstruse and untenable arguments.

There are, indeed, hundreds of sceptics, and inveterate ones, too, who have never turned their attention in the slightest degree to science; how much more likely is it, then, that there may be those who, being already sceptical, direct their study to science for no other purpose than laying hold of the most salient points for the gratification of manifesting to the world their impious principles? However, there are many writers of the present day who, without laying themselves open to this charge, have erred, and widely, in their dealings with Scripture and science.

The " Mosaic Cosmogony " in the " Essays and Reviews " is compounded of arguments as futile, short-sighted, and untenable as any we have heard; and although anything like an investigation of them, as an answer to that essay, cannot be attempted by us here, still we shall note a few, simply for the purpose of exposing their weakness and unplausibility.

The writer, commencing with some remarks respecting Galileo and the introduction of the Copernican system of astronomy, touching the immobility of the earth, says :—" The solution of the difficulty offered by Galileo and others was, that the object of a revelation, or divine unveiling of mysteries, must be to teach man things which he is unable and must ever remain unable to find out for himself; but not physical truths, for the discovery of which he has faculties specially provided by his Creator. Hence it was not unreasonable, that, in regard to matters of fact merely, the sacred writers should use the common language and assume the common belief of mankind, without purporting to correct errors upon points morally indifferent. So, in regard to such a text as

' The world is established, it cannot be moved,' though it might imply the sacred penman's ignorance of the fact that the earth does move, yet it does not put forth this opinion as an indispensable point of faith. And this remark is applicable to a number of texts which present a similar difficulty." Could, we ask, any reasoning be more unphilosophical in its application, or more damaging to religion ? In the first place it supposes the inspired writers to be, somehow or other, half inspired, revealing important *truths* which men cannot find out for themselves; but when the same writers touch on those things which men's faculties enable them to judge the truth of, then their inspiration is mixed with error. The idea is positively ridiculous. With regard to the text spoken of, " The world is established, it cannot be moved," the writer speaks of the ignorance of the " sacred penman " of the fact that the earth *does* move. We by no means see the necessity of this assumed ignorance. Truly the world is established— established in its course round the sun, and from which course it cannot be moved or turned. The text may with equal propriety be rendered thus, or we have altogether mistaken the use and application of words. In fact, it is the splitting of such straws as these that make up the chief of the arguments used by this class of writers.

The writer, speaking of the first chapter of Genesis, says, "It can scarcely be said that this chapter is not intended, in part, to teach and convey at least some physical truth (we should think so); and taking its words in their plain sense," the writer continues, "it manifestly gives a view of the universe adverse to that of modern science." It will be seen from our essay " On the Six Days of Creation," to which we refer our readers, how far we feel inclined to admit the *latter* part of the writer's statement.

The essayist, after a few introductory remarks on geology, &c., and briefly touching on the Hebrew word (*bara*,) which, as he affirms, may not simply mean created from nothing, but may also mean to shape from pre-existing matter, commences his criticism with the introduction of light on the first day,* which he

---

* We do not believe, with several eminent writers, that the light on the first day emanated from the sun, but that it had a distinct and separate existence. To suppose that the light arose from the partial clearing away of mists which hung thickly round the earth, is to our mind very repugnant, and does great injury not only to the simple words, "And God saw the light that it was good," but also to the fourth day's creation, which, although the body of the sun may not have been created then, the light certainly was.

considers "repugnant to our modern know-ledge," but which we feel more inclined to attribute to our want of sufficient knowledge to be enabled to understand the passage correctly. (*See Essay "On the Six Days of Creation."*) He says, " Thus light and the measurement of time are represented as existing before the manifestation of the sun." We would invite him to study the passage more closely, and show us where the measurement of time is spoken of, before the " manifestation of the sun " on the fourth day. Truly, the "*evening and the morning*" are spoken of as constituting the "*first day;*" but, we ask, would it not be by far the most reasonable—especially when the claims of science demand it—to regard these expressions as figurative ?—and which we may do, without doing any violence to the inspired record, or injuring the sense of its interpreta-tion. Indeed, there cannot be a shadow of a doubt remaining to those who have well studied the subject, that the *days* spoken of refer to indefinite but immense periods of time. Against this it is argued that the expression, " the evening and the morning "—the Hebrew way of reckoning the day—would indicate an ordinary day, but we cannot see the necessity at all. We speak of the evening of life and the morning of life, which, in fact, constitute man's *day*, but at the same time a life-time; we also speak of the evening of an age, and which more nearly approaches the subject; but it were too absurd in either case to suppose it bore reference to a period of twenty-four hours. Besides all which, three days of creation had actually passed before the manifestation of the sun and moon, which were to be " for signs and for seasons, and for *days*, and years." Are we, then, to suppose that these intervals were marked off in exactly the same way before, as after the introduction of that which was to govern them and denote their duration? It is not impossible, we admit; at the same time, it seems in the highest degree improbable.

The writer, speaking of the second day's creation, says, " The work of the second day of creation is to erect the vault of heaven (Hebrew, *rakia*; Greek, στερέωμα; Latin, *firmamentum*), which is represented as supporting an ocean of water above it. The waters are said to be divided, so that some are below, some above the vault. That the Hebrews understood the sky, firmament, or heaven, to be a permanent, solid vault, as it appears to the ordinary observer, is evident enough from various expressions made use of concerning it. It is said to have pillars (Job xxvi. 2), foundations (2 Sam. xxii. 8), doors (Ps. lxxviii. 23), and windows (Gen. vii. 11). No quibbling about the derivation of the word *rakia*, which is, literally, something beaten out, can affect the explicit description of the Mosaic writer, contained in the words ' the waters that are above the firmament,' or avail to show that he was aware that the sky is but transparent space."

Now, without wishing to have any "*quibbling*" respecting the derivation of words, we must admit that there is some difficulty here to contend with; and, so far as we are able to judge, about the only one we can find worth noticing. But we must at the same time avow our opinion, that the difficulty does not lie in the narrative itself, but from a thorough want of knowledge—we may say, entire ignorance—of the subject, *which future revelations and discoveries of science may supply.* We coincide with Buckland, to a great extent, when he says, " After all, it should be recollected that the question is not respecting the correctness of the Mosaic narrative, but of our interpretation of it," and that is where so much mischief lies, in the *mis-interpretation* of the Scriptures ; in support of which we have only to call attention to the passages referred to in the extract we have just given, and which are quoted without any reference to the context, which would, to say the least of it, greatly modify, if not altogether destroy, the meaning sought to be given to it by the writer, which our readers will find on referring themselves.

The only objection which the writer seems to raise respecting the third day's creation is, that mention is only made of the fact that "the earth brought forth grass, *and* herb yielding seed, and the tree yielding fruit," on this day, and which productions are spoken of afterwards—(Gen. i. 29)—as being given to man for food, while no mention is made of other vegetable productions "not serviceable to this purpose." The writer then seems half inclined to explain the seeming omission, in saying that "perhaps it may be contended— since there is no vegetable production which may not possibly be useful to man, or which is not preyed upon by some animal—that in this description the whole terrestrial flora is implied." We are of opinion, that the whole of the *then existing* flora is implied, and which included the various ferns, reeds, &c., that form the substance of our coal-measures; and although no notice is given of the fact, it is our opinion that higher and higher organisa- tions were developed in progression as age after age rolled by;* and although, when man

* We may remark that the Mosaic description of creation gives only the most striking results of creation

was ushered in, the flora might still possess many of its *former* characteristics, which must have been luxurious in the extreme from the still retained heat of the earth, yet there is no doubt that it had attained a much higher stage of development, and exhibited many modifications in form and structure, arising to a great extent from the cooler condition of the earth's surface. The fourth and fifth days are passed over by the writer in a somewhat cursory manner, from which we conclude, he finds nothing strikingly antagonistic contained in the account.

He then proceeds, after remarking on the creation of the beast in the former part of the sixth day, with the account of the creation of man, as follows :—" The formation of man is distinguished by a variation of the creative fiat. 'Let us make man in our image, after our likeness.' Accordingly, man is made and formed (*bara*) in the image and likeness of God; a phrase which has been explained away to mean merely ' perfect, sinless,' although the Pentateuch abounds in passages showing that the Hebrews contemplated the Divine Being in the visible form of a man."

which distinguish each successive day, without entering into any detail respecting their succeeding development.

We do not exactly understand the writer's object in this extract, as we have never yet seen the necessity of regarding the " Divine Being" otherwise than as existing in the *visible form of a man*, whatever *modern spiritualism* may endeavour to prove to the contrary; Scripture abounds with passages in support of this from beginning to end. The writer then proceeds :—" Man is said to have been created male and female, and the narrative contains nothing to show that a single pair only is intended. It is in the second narrative of creation that the formation of a single man out of the dust of the earth is described, and the omission to create a female at the same time, is stated to have been repaired by the subsequent formation of one from the side of the man."

With regard to the simultaneous creation of man, male and female, spoken of in the first chapter of Genesis, there is nothing, we admit, " to show that a single pair only is intended;" indeed, there seems every probability that there were more. But, in admitting this, we must avow our belief that this account bears no reference to that given of the formation of Adam in the second chapter. We are led, in fact, to assign to the man of the sixth day's creation a Pre-Adamic existence, and to regard the two accounts given as referring to two distinct and separate events. (*See "Essay on the Probability of the Existence of Man before Adam."*) The writer of the essay on the "Mosaic Cosmogony" has, like the majority of people, confounded the two accounts, as referring to one and the same event; and which, in this instance, we are sorry to add, has induced the writer to use language, to say the least of it, derogatory to the wisdom and excellence of the Deity. He accuses God of downright short-sightedness, and there can be no misunderstanding his words; we repeat them. He says, "The *omission* to create a female at the same time"—speaking of the formation of Adam—"is stated to have been *repaired* by the subsequent formation of one from the side of the man." The omission and reparation are too plainly spoken of to admit of any other construction being placed upon them.

After a few further remarks on the old controversy respecting the carnivorous animals,* and briefly noticing the conclusion of the "nar-

---

* Objections have been raised relative to the existence of the carnivorous animals, or *flesh-eaters*—first, because no distinct account is given of their creation; and, secondly, because in Gen. i. 30, God is said to "have given to the beast of the earth" every green herb for meat!

rative" and the "Sabbatic rest," the writer then commences an investigation of the various theories propounded by Buckland, Chalmers, Hugh Miller, and others, in explanation of the Mosaic account, and so continues to the end of his essay. We, however, cannot follow him further; we have already exceeded our intended limits, and in doing so have gone over the principal objections he has raised; and trust, in the essays we have written *devoted to this subject,* to be enabled to show still more clearly how untenable, in the majority of cases, are the arguments made use of against the *inspired record.*

The first, second, and third essays of our series are devoted more particularly to the investigation of the Mosaic account of creation, which we have just been briefly considering in connexion with the essay on the "Mosaic Cosmogony," published with, and forming part of, the "Essays and Reviews."

The fourth essay, "On the Physical Constitution of the Universe," touches on the various sciences and their teachings, with inquiries concerning the elementary character of matter, showing the fallacy of the elements of the ancients, and the important office fulfilled by some of the elementary bodies in the constitution of matter.

The fifth essay, "On Matter and its Properties," commences with an investigation of the atomic theory and the infinite divisibility of matter, and is devoted more particularly to the examination of the various properties of matter, with some concluding remarks on motion and forces.

The sixth essay, " On the Immensity of the Universe," contains a detailed account of the solar system, with a general description of the heavenly bodies, showing their magnitude, and the unbounded vastness of the celestial spaces. It may be regarded as introductory to the seventh and final essay, " On the Multiplicity of Worlds," the last of our series, which contains a careful investigation of the various arguments used for and against the probability of other inhabited worlds, we, at the same time, supporting the theory, feeling assured that nothing can be found that can properly be regarded as antagonistic, whether philosophically or biblically considered, as we trust our arguments will prove. Indeed, we find abundant passages throughout Scripture which not only favour the idea, but will scarcely admit of any other interpretation being placed upon them. The essay concludes with the consideration of man's future home in the universe.

In concluding these introductory remarks, we invite the reader's careful and unbiassed consideration of the various subjects, and if we can be proved to have erred in the treatment of any of them, we shall warmly and gratefully receive and acknowledge any communications that may be the means of setting us right. But we must repeat, in connexion with Scripture, that whatever interpretation is placed upon it, must be in accordance with, and not antagonistic to, its teachings — *God's works cannot contradict His words.*

ESSAY I.

ON THE FORMATION OF THE WORLD.

Matter unformed and void : darkness profound
Covered the abyss ; but on the watery calm
His brooding wings the Spirit of God outspread,
And vital virtue infused, and vital warmth,
Thoughout the fluid mass : but downward purged
The black, tartareous, cold, infernal dregs,
Adverse to life : then founded, then conglobed
Like things to like ; the rest to several place
Disparted ; and, between, spun out the air :
And earth, self-balanced, on her centre hung.
                                        MILTON.

THE consideration of a subject manifestly so
full of interest as the formation of the world,
and its preparation for the reception of inhabitants, cannot fail, we imagine, to command

B

the attention of any one taking the slightest
degree of interest in the investigation of truth,
and the tracing of events to their primary
causes.

We are aware, by many these investigations
are looked upon as being presumptuous and
beyond the limits of human understanding ;
we, however, think otherwise, and even go so
far as to believe that it is almost a part of our
duty to do so, being especially constituted and
adapted in our present state for the study of
the material universe in general, whether it be
in the geological relics of the past, in the
heavens above, in the air which surrounds us,
or in any other displays of nature with which
we are acquainted. How far we may be allowed
to prosecute the same inquiries in our future
state is not seen; certain it is, we have this
privilege now—for privilege we must insist on
its being termed, and doubtless intended for
us to make use of.

The formation of the world, which, in fact,
constitutes the study of geology, appears to
have been regarded, generally, in rather an
unfavourable light, in its bearing upon revelation. This fact is mainly due from inferences
drawn from too hasty conclusions being arrived
at in the study of a science still in its infancy.
We do not mean by that to infer that any

great alterations in the general principles of geology will ever take place, but future knowledge may considerably modify many existing theories concerning them. We also consider many writers have been much to blame in the careless manner in which they have passed over and endeavoured to reconcile the seeming contradictions and discrepancies arising therefrom, when a more careful study of the subject in its religious relations might have set the matter right, and would have been received more favourably, not only by those who make it more particularly their study, but the world generally; for, notwithstanding the many narrow-minded, although doubtless well-meaning people, who set their faces against such investigations, people generally have shown themselves deeply interested with the results; and among the many false notions which they have assumed is, that geologists generally have turned the results of their labours against revelation, and so endeavouring to falsify its teachings and authority. Nothing could possibly be more unfounded and untrue; indeed, many who have shown themselves most eminent in the study of geology, have been men of the strictest piety, and possessing the greatest possible reverence to the inspiration of the word of God; and who have sought the science rather as an interpreter to the Scriptures, than as a refuter; and so it is. Properly regarded and understood, geology should be the sister-study to the Bible, explaining its grandest truths and making intelligible the most wonderful and absorbing passages. On the other hand—we regret to say it—it is undoubtedly the stanchest friends of the Bible who have done it the most mischief by proclaiming, as hostile, the simple though grand teachings of geology. As an illustration take, for instance, the supposed great age of the world. Now, simply because the history of man only extends back some six thousand years, from the time, in fact, when Adam was placed upon it, and because geology points to an age, or rather ages of ages, the contemplation of which overwhelms the mind from its immense continuity;—because such is the case, it is considered hostile to the Word of God, when a proper study of the first verse in that Book would settle the question at once. "In the beginning God created the heaven and the earth." "When?" we ask: and show us who will answer our question chronologically; it may have been millions upon millions of years ere our first parent Adam was placed upon it; and it not only may be so, but doubtless was.

It has been said, "the proper study for mankind, is man;" and to a large extent this is very true. But, in allowing such, we must admit that when properly regarded, it necessitates also the study of the material world on which he exists, and even in these prescribed limits we find no barrier to the contemplation of this subject. And furthermore, the important facts which modern investigations have disclosed concerning the various strata which constitute the crust of the world, and the insight they give us as to the condition of the earth for ages antecedent to the creation of man, have gone far to render the study of geological research one of the most absorbing and interesting branches of human knowledge.

Scarcely fifty years have elapsed since the attention of scientific men was first directed to the various rocks and stratifications which present themselves in different parts of the earth's surface. Mr. Robert Bakewell seems to have been the first in England to devote his time to the cultivation of this science, and in 1814 published a book entitled "Introduction to Geology," which was the first work exclusively devoted to this subject, and formed the basis of all subsequent works on this branch of knowledge; and many of our most eminent geologists of the present day are indebted to this book for the groundwork of their information. Since then, however, many able and learned investigators have contributed largely by their writings and labours to extend our knowledge concerning the structure of the earth, together with the organic fossilized remains imbedded therein.

It is not our intention, however, to follow minutely these investigations, or enter into lengthy discussions regarding the various theories which from time to time have been propounded; although at times it will be necessary for us to enter into an explanation of the causes that have produced the various phenomena which are exhibited by the different rocks and stratifications, as much of the interest connected with the study of geology is derived from speculations of this nature.

Our more immediate purpose, however, is to endeavour to investigate, in as intelligible a manner as possible, the condition of the earth in the beginning, and the causes which have influenced the production of the various rocks and stratifications which form the crust of the earth. In these investigations the geologist actually becomes the physical geographer of former worlds, whose animals have lived, died, and become fossilized and entombed; and whose remains will for ever perpetuate the knowledge that they, like us, once lived and flourished. For whilst the geographer now draws maps and charts of continents and oceans, lakes and rivers, the geologist on the other hand marks out where oceans and lakes once covered the land, where rivers in countless ages back fertilized the soil, and where extensive forests once flourished in gorgeous magnificence. He is enabled to trace footprints on the sands, and the ripples of the water on the now indurated beech; and in some instances the impression of rain-drops has been preserved—telling us that then, as now, the earth received the grateful showers from the clouds.

The first verse of the first chapter of the Book of Genesis—as all are aware—reads thus: "In the beginning God created the heaven and the earth." Now, by many, and we may say the majority of people, this passage is regarded as referring to a period of six of our days before the creation, or rather formation of Adam. The absurdity of this supposition we shall at once endeavour to demonstrate. First of all, we have definitely to inquire as to what is really meant by a day, as spoken of in various passages of Scripture. And perhaps one of the most striking passages occurs in the third chapter of the second epistle of Peter, at the eighth verse: "But, beloved, be not ignorant of this one thing, that one day is with the Lord as a thousand years, and a thousand years as one day." This text alone serves to show what an indefinite period a day may represent. It does not teach us that whenever a day is spoken of in Scripture it refers to a thousand years, but it does teach us that a day in the sight of God may embrace a period infinitely greater than our ordinary conceptions would lead us to attribute to it.

In Daniel, for instance, xxxiv. 8, we read: "For it is the day of the Lord's vengeance, and the year of recompences for the controversy of Zion." Now in this we have a day, and a year, spoken of as referring to the same period, and duration of time. Why, then, should not the days spoken of in Genesis refer to longer periods than twenty-four hours? Here, too, another difficulty presents itself, for we must remember that during the first three days of creation there was neither sun nor moon; for even though these huge masses of matter were created in the beginning, and simultaneously with the earth, yet it was not till the fourth day that God made the sun "to give light upon the earth." Now, as what we generally understand as a day, comprehends the lapse of time between the rising and setting of the sun, we are at a loss to know—in the absence of that luminary—how the duration of the day was measured. And from this we must come to the conclusion that the days spoken of in Genesis must refer to periods greatly differing from half the revolution of the earth on its axis. Thus, then, it becomes evident that the beginning of the creation of the material universe—judging alone from Scripture—could not have taken place six of our days before the peopling of the earth with man. When, however, we bring science and the testimony of the rocks to bear upon it, it places the matter beyond further doubt, and tells us, in unmistakeable language, the immensity and continuity of those days, or cycles of ages, during which time creation was being completed. In what light, then, shall we regard those three words, " In the beginning ? " or to what periods are we to suppose they refer ? To solve this question chronologically we would not attempt, feeling sure that all inquiries of this description would be met by vexation and disappointment, inasmuch as nothing could be more indefinite than the statement as it stands. It is independent and isolated from all that comes after; it seems to have no connexion at all with the operations of the Creator on the first day. It has, indeed, been usually understood that the beginning spoken of by Moses, is so connected with the six days' work, that we must regard it as coeval with the first of those days ; and if those be regarded as literal days, and the chronology of man as reaching back only about six thousand years, the beginning must have been nearly of the same age. But it can never be proved that the days were not separated from the beginning by an indefinite interval. If so, that interval may have been incalculably long, —long enough to satisfy all the demands of geology.[*]

How far back, in the eternity of the past, shapeless matter may have held its place, we do not know, and probably never shall. What condition it occupied in the infinity of space, whether in huge formless masses, still and motionless, or in gigantic clouds of nebulous matter floating in the dark infinitude, seems also equally difficult to determine, although it is well worthy of consideration.

However, before proceeding further, we must call attention to the difficulty amongst theologians respecting the Hebrew word (*bara*) " created," which, they say, does not necessarily mean to make out of nothing, but may also mean to form from matter already existing. This we must regard as purely speculative, as

* Hitchcock's " Religion of Geology."

it may or may not be the case; but certainly
neither one way nor the other will interfere
with its scientific bearing. Although it must
be evident that if matter existed previous to
the creation described in the first verse of
Genesis, then must matter be co-eternal with
the Creator, inasmuch as were it otherwise the
original creation of matter would be the
beginning, and not its after formation into the
heavens and the earth; which would be a con-
tradiction and an absurdity, without we regard the word " beginning " as referring to the
commencement of the *organization* of the pre-
existing matter. However, as we have before
said, it does not immediately concern the
subject under consideration. The question is,
what was the probable condition of matter in
the beginning, whenever that was ?

Now it is proposed by the supporters of the
nebular hypothesis, that the entire universe,
in the beginning, was composed of this
nebulous matter, and that in accordance with
a great law of nature one particle attracted
another, which became a centre for condensation, which, by increasing in size, became a
sun, or central orb of condensations of a
similar character, which formed the planets.
Such was the theory introduced by that celebrated astronomer La Place, and, ingenious as

it. is, yet there are many objections to its reception. And in the first place this theory will admit of no other supposition than that the earth and all the other planets, from the beginning of creation, must have assumed a globular form. Now this is directly antagonistic to Scripture, according to its literal translation, for we read distinctly that the earth was *without form;* this, therefore, would appear the greatest drawback to the theory as it now stands.

But many interpreters do not give to this expression the chaotic character which has so long prevailed. Thus writes Dr. Hitchcock, in his " Religion of Geology," page 178 :— " Among all heathen nations of antiquity, the belief in a primeval chaos was almost universal, and from the heathen philosophers it was transmitted to the Christian world, and incorporated with the Mosaic cosmogony. It is not, indeed, easy to ascertain what is the precise idea which has been attached to a chaos. It is generally described, however, as a ' confused assemblage of elements,' ' an unformed and undigested mass of heterogeneous matter ;' not, of course, subject to those laws which now govern it, and which have arranged it all in beautiful order, even if we leave out of the account vegetable and animal organization.

Now, I have attempted to show that there never was a period on the globe when these laws, with the exception of the organic, did not operate as they now do. Nay, the geologist, when he examines the oldest rocks, finds the results of these laws at the supposed period when chaos reigned, that is, in the earliest times of our planet. And what are these results? The most splendid crystallizations which nature furnishes. The emerald, the topaz, the sapphire, and other kindred gems, were elaborated during the supposed chaotic state of the globe; for no earlier products have yet been discovered than these most perfect illustrations of crystallographical, chemical, and electrical laws. If, indeed, any should say, that by a chaos they mean only that state of the world when no animals or planets existed, in other words, when no organic laws had been established—to such a chaos I have no objection. And this is the chaos described in the Bible, when it is said that, before the creation of animals and plants, the earth was without form and void. The ' tohu vau bohu ' of Moses, which is thus translated in our English Bibles, means, simply and literally, *invisible and unfurnished—invisible*, both because the ocean covered the present land, and darkness was upon the face of the deep; and *unfurnished*, because as yet no organic natures had been called into existence."

So far, however, as these opinions of Dr. Hitchcock are concerned, and which to a very great extent we subscribe, they would rather support than interfere with the hypothesis of La Place. There are objections, however, of a very different character, which appear of much greater importance as affecting the laws of Newton.

Theory would suggest that in any nebulous mass, however great, the point of condensation and attraction would be the centre, and there only. Indeed, the laws of universal gravitation, according to the philosophy of Newton, will admit of no other speculation. This being the case, the whole would have condensed in one mass; there could not have been a separate centre for each individual planet and satellite.

The further consideration of this subject has suggested an alteration which will, we think, adequately meet the objections we have just raised, both with regard to Scripture and science. We must admit that we always have regarded with aversion the idea of the creation of unmeaning and formless lumps of conglomerated masses of matter; it appears to partake of so little of the symmetry and perfection universally displayed in the works of the all-wise and omnipotent Creator, that we have always regarded it with doubt and uncertainty.

We have been placed as it were between two fires; on the one hand, we have had a theory possessing a great deal of ingenuity but antagonistic to revealed truth, whilst on the other hand we have a theory which, although meeting the objection of the former one, supplies us with one which has not even the merit of symmetry, much less that ideal perfection which characterizes the Most High.

Let us, then, assume that the nebular hypothesis is correct, so far as the original creation of matter is concerned, and that the consolidation commenced at a point occupying the centre of the nebulæ. Now there can be no doubt that, simultaneously with the creation of matter, God instituted all the laws that were to govern it; and, that being the case, particles when brought together would exercise their chemical affinity for each other. This, as is well known, cannot take place without the evolution of heat; this heat, as further condensation went on, would become greater and greater, and would ultimately develop itself as fire—there can be little doubt—and so continue until the whole nebulous mass had condensed; after which time the exterior would gradually become cool and solid. In this condition it may have remained for ages, its surface becoming more and more cool and hard, but nevertheless working within itself its predestined destruction. We can readily conceive that, with the raging fires, chemical unions and decompositions, that explosive gases were generated on an alarming scale, and there entombed and compressed were groaning for liberation.

At length the time for the grand phenomena arrives, and with a burst that reverberates almost to infinitude the ponderous mass is shattered, and the formless lumps are hurled into their appointed places. We say formless, as there can be no doubt that the crust which composed the enormous globe, on being broken up, would assume every fantastic shape, without any form in particular—in short, no more nor less than formless—and in this condition would gradually cool; and we may suppose that this was the state of our earth at the commencement of the first day, submerged beneath the waters produced upon its surface by the condensing of the vapours, arising from the long-continued union of the oxygen and hydrogen, during the enormous combustion of the elements.

We are not aware of any such theory as the foregoing having been proposed before, but it appears to us to meet the requirements of the

`case better than any other with which we are
acquainted. Even the present condition of the
earth will in a great measure support the supposition; in fact, it represents in miniature
the condition of the ponderous mass we have
just been speaking of, with only this difference,
that the hard indurated crust of the earth—
which encloses the fiery mass—is covered with
stratified and sedimentary rocks of an entirely
different character, which must have been produced by the continued action of the waters,
which detaching the substance of the rocks in
the form of a fine powder, was deposited at the
bottom, and so became stratified and hardened;
and so on and on through successive ages,
entombing and fossilizing the various orders of
animals that were successively produced; and
it is more than probable that all the planets
which compose our system are similarly
situated, although it may be in various stages
of development.

An interesting field for inquiry is opened
up by the consideration of the probability that
the position of the asteroids was once occupied
by a single large planet, which may have
shared the fate that we have assigned to the
conglobed mass in the first instance, and which
warns us that a like fate may await the earth.
It may, it is true, have been dashed into

C

fragments by collision with a comet; it seems
more probable, however, that it was caused by
some internal volcanic agency, especially when
we consider that the theory respecting the
physical constitution of comets has been of
such a very doubtful character, many regarding
them as little else than huge nebulous masses;
and although we feel inclined to differ on this
point, still we consider it far less probable that
the origin of the asteroids was due to the
collision of a comet with a primary planet, than
that it arose from the bursting open of the
planet from the imprisonment of long accumulated and explosive gases. This will receive
further support from the fact, that the bursting
of anything arising from explosion within, has
a tendency to scatter the fragments in every
possible direction. Take, for instance, that
destructive agent of modern warfare, the bomb-
shell—see how it bursts and scatters its fiery
missiles in a thousand different directions; now
this is exactly what we find to be the case with
respect to the asteroids. " These bodies," says
Dr. Lardner, "which have been called planetoids or asteroids, obey the law of gravitation in
their motion round the sun. Their distances
from that luminary are not only different one
from another, but they differ from all the other
planets in their extremely small magnitude.

In the telescope they are seen as stars of the tenth or twelfth magnitude, and their real magnitudes are so minute that they have never yet been certainly ascertained, notwithstanding the number and power of the telescopes that have been directed to them."

As to the origin of comets we have never heard anything definitely expressed, but we are of opinion that they were produced con- temporary with the planets; and it is for us now to advance a theory in explanation of this statement, and to do this we must return to the time when we have supposed the original mass of matter to have been broken up.

Now, it is well known that a force sufficient to project a given weight to a certain distance, would project a much smaller weight to a much greater distance; the ratio of the distance increasing inversely with the reduction of the weight projected. This being the case, the smaller lumps of matter, which doubtless must have detached themselves from the greater masses during explosion, would have been hurled into space to far greater distances, and in true keeping with the universal law of gravitation, might have assumed both the parabolic and hyperbolic orbits.

It has been shown by Newton, that if a body move in a certain form of curve, called

by geometers a conic section, having a point
called its focus at the centre of the sun, it
must be subject to the attraction of the sun's
gravitation, and it must reciprocally attract
the sun.   Now, these comets have been ascertained by observation to move in these very
curves, the sun being in their common focus ;
hence, they and the sun mutually attract each
other according to the universal law of gravitation.   They are, therefore, masses of ponderable matter.   But these masses are not only
attracted by the sun but by the planets,
primary and secondary, near to which they
pass ; and they are ascertained to deviate considerably, by reason of such attractions, from
the paths they would follow if subject only to
the sun's attractive force. Now by the general
law of gravitation, that attraction is always
reciprocal, and it is certain that the comets
attract the planets as strongly as the planets
attract them ; and if the masses of the comets
were as great as those of the planets, they
would cause the planets to deviate from their
accustomed path as widely as the planets cause
them to deviate.   If, however, we find that
while the deviation of the comets, in virtue of
this mutual attraction, is very great, that of
the planets is extremely small, the inference
must be that the masses of the comets are

smaller than those of the planets, in exactly the proportion in which the effect of the attraction on the planet is less than its effect upon the comet. Now, in fact, it has been found that while the deviation of the comets, due to the attractions of the planets, is very considerable, that of the planets, of the satellites, and even of the planetoids—the smallest bodies of the solar system—is so minute as to be absolutely inappreciable by the most exact means of observation. A case is even recorded in which a comet passed almost in contact with the satellites of Jupiter, if, indeed, it did not pass among those small bodies ; yet its attraction upon them was so feeble as to produce not the slightest observable effect upon their motions, although the comet itself, by the attraction of the planet, was so strongly affected that its orbit was completely changed. By such observations and calculations it has then been established, that although the comets are masses of ponderable matter, the quantity of matter composing each of them is incalculably less than that of the smallest planet, primary or secondary, of the solar system.* In the present essay we have not confined ourselves exclusively to the consideration of the earth, but have extended

* Lardner's "Museum of Science," &c.—Vol. II., p. 68.

our study rather to the beginning of the
material universe in general, as much as anything, from the fact that the first verse in
Genesis leads us to suppose that the heaven
and the earth were of simultaneous origin, and
as such we have endeavoured to explain the
various causes which may have influenced the
beginning of creation in producing the results
which are constantly under our observation.

Regarding the fixed stars and the various
nebulæ which are visible, either with or without the telescope, we have no hesitation in
saying that their origin must be precisely
similar to, and contemporary with, the sun and
the solar system; but they need not necessarily
be in exactly the same condition, although it
is probable many of them are. It would
appear that considerable doubt exists respecting some nebulæ which have not been resolved
into separate stars by the telescope; but considering that in the majority of cases they have
been found to be resolvable, we imagine it
only to be a question of telescopes of sufficient
power to resolve the others. We do not
believe any of them to be in the same nebulous
state as we have just been considering to be
the primary condition of matter, for more than
one obvious reason. In the first place, we
should not imagine that matter in this con-

dition could be self-luminous; and in the next place, even though it were luminous, it would certainly not be visible to us at the distance which is generally assigned to them; for if the accumulated light from thousands—it may be millions of bright and gorgeous suns—when so far removed, is so faint that it is scarcely perceptible to the unassisted eye, how shall we expect that the feeble light which might stream from a filmy nebula could reach us? There is, then, no alternative but to admit that each individual nebula consists of a galaxy of innumerable suns, perhaps as far exceeding our sun in splendour as our sun does its lesser light, the moon, and each, too, perhaps the centre of a system of planets.

The idea is overwhelming, we admit, and even humiliating to man's pride; he would fain place the world, as did the ancient astronomers, as the centre of the universe, and regard the myriad starry host as mere lamps and ornaments hung there just to relieve the midnight gloom. Truly they fill this office well; but far more noble is their use, and far higher their destiny, and ages after ages may roll on in the long eternity to come, ere we shall begin to comprehend the vastness of this great infinitude.

ESSAY II.

ON THE SIX DAYS OF CREATION.

FORM OF THE EARTH—EARTH SUBMERGED—INTRODUCTION
OF LIGHT ON THE FIRST DAY—AURORA BOREALIS—
SECOND DAY—PRIMARY ROCKS—DAWN OF LIFE—THIRD
DAY'S CREATION—DRY LAND—DEVONIAN SYSTEM—COOL
STRATAS—FOURTH DAY—THE SUN AND MOON—INCAN-
DESCENT SOLAR ATMOSPHERE — FOOTPRINTS — FIFTH
DAY—OOLITIC SYSTEM—SIXTH DAY—THE BEAST OF THE
EARTH—MAN.

IN the consideration of this subject we shall
take it for granted that the days spoken of by
Moses are not, what has been so generally but
absurdly supposed, days of twenty-four hours'
duration, but periods in conformity with the
testimony of the rocks and the study of
geology; periods in which the handiwork of
the great Creator was progressing with a slow
but grand development. It may be that the
simplicity of the account given by Moses has
been the cause, to some extent, of the aversion

to regard the days there spoken of as lengthened
periods of time ; there is a promptness in the
description of the fulfilment of the commands
of the Creator which favours the idea of a
speedy and almost instantaneous transition
and completeness. As an instance, take the
expression, " Let there be light : and there
was light." There seems to be in this an immediate compliance with the command. And
yet actually, with regard to time, nothing could
be more indefinite than its fulfilment ; it
might just as well have occupied a thousand
years as a single second. Indeed, the question
of time is left out entirely—there is simply the
fact of a command given and of its being
obeyed ; but what space of time was occupied
is not mentioned, either in this one particular
instance or any of the succeeding accounts of
creation, excepting, of course, the days already
spoken of. Supposing, however, we were
inclined to admit the probability of the instantaneous accomplishment of the Creator's
commands, which by no means we are, then
we cannot conceive why even the space of
twenty-four hours was required. The idea
seems too absurd to indulge in for a single
moment, that God should give a command,
which was instantly fulfilled, and then leave
the scene of His *labours* (we say labours, ad-

visedly) for twenty-four hours, then re-visit it, issue another command, which would be equally quickly fulfilled, and then retire from the scene again; and so on to the completion of creation. The absurdity of such an idea must be manifest to every one who can think and read. God might have issued His commands in a single hour (aye, less) if they were fulfilled as quickly as this, which would have been the death-blow to a certain excessively common expression, "The world was not made in a day."

As our investigations must be searching, we shall have to enter somewhat into the detail of the description given by Moses; and we therefore think it better to give the original text of each day's creation as we come to it, and examine each separately, commencing with the first five verses in Genesis, containing the description of the first day.

Genesis i. 1 to 5.—" In the beginning God created the heaven and the earth. And the earth was without form and void; and darkness was upon the face of the deep. And the Spirit of God moved upon the face of the waters. And God said, Let there be light; and there was light. And God saw the light that it was good; and God divided the light from the darkness. And God called the light Day, and the darkness He called Night. And the evening and the morning were the first day."

Of course, the first verse is a simple statement of God's having created heaven and the earth in the beginning, but which, at the same time, unmistakeably implies that all the heavenly bodies, including the earth, are of simultaneous origin. We would here remark, however, that this first verse must be dissociated from that which follows, and does not bear any reference to the first day.

The second verse opens with a negative description of the earth at the commencement of the first day, " without form and void." At one time we were disposed to regard this as referring to the absence of light, as, of course, without light there could be no form to anything; but on further study we were convinced that this could not refer to the absence of light, as in conjunction with the above passage we read, that " darkness was upon the face of the deep," thus indicating the non-existence of light. Therefore the alternative was interpreting the passage literally, that the earth was without form. The study of this subject led us into many perplexing inquiries, not the least of which was, how to reconcile the formless condition of the earth with the universally received laws which govern the heavenly bodies, which laws require that the earth would speedily have assumed the spheroidal form, that is, in exactly the same shape as we know it to be now; but the objection was overcome by regarding the passage as referring, not to the earth with continents and oceans as we now know it, but to the solid earth only, which then must have occupied the centre of an immense sphere of water, and under such circumstances might have continued in the formless condition we read of.

Of the immensity of the water which existed in this condition of the earth we have abundant proofs from Scripture, and it is also equally certain that the earth was entirely submerged, else, why the command on the third day for the dry land to appear? And doubtless it was during this time that the first of the primary rocks were being formed.

The rock which is generally found resting on granite, very much resembles it in its formation, and must have been disintegrated particles of granite deposited by aqueous suspension. Granite, we need scarcely add, being the last of the rock formations, formed by the gradual cooling of its constituent elements from a state of incandescence.

Having made these few remarks with reference to the condition of the earth prior to the creation or calling forth of light, we have now to consider the nature and introduction of the light created, for we must remember that it was not until the fourth day that God caused the sun and moon to send forth their lights. We read, " that darkness was upon the face of the deep," and that " the Spirit of God moved upon the face of the waters." Nothing is said as to how the light was produced, but this passage would almost induce us to believe that it originated in some manner from the waters; how, it is impossible to say. Perhaps from some electric phenomena with which we are unacquainted, but which might have encircled the watery globe as a luminous band. There is something singular about this also, inasmuch as no account is given of the withdrawal of this light, after the introduction of the light from the sun and moon. May we be allowed to suggest that it never was entirely withdrawn, and that the remaining vestiges may be traced in part to the beautiful aurora which more northern nations are constantly privileged to witness.

There is something really beautiful in this theory, we think, when placed side by side with the challenge of God to Job, as follows (Job xxxviii. 19—24):—" Where is the way where light dwelleth? and as for darkness, where is the place thereof? That thou shouldest take it to the bound thereof, and that thou shouldest know the paths to the house thereof? (Knowest thou it, because thou wast then born? or because the number of thy days is great?) Hast thou entered into the treasures of the snow? or hast thou seen the treasures of the hail, which I have reserved against the time of trouble, against the day of battle and war? By what way is the light parted, which scattereth the east wind upon the earth?"

There is something very striking in these passages, and it would take more time than we can devote here to attempt to offer even a partial explanation of them, although a few remarks on the more prominent features connected with them may not be out of place.

In the first instance, God demands of Job, "Where is the way where light dwelleth?" Now, although we would not presume to give any positive answer to this question—a question which God put to Job to convince him of ignorance—yet it must be clear to all, that it could not refer to the light we receive from the sun, otherwise there could have been no difficulty whatever in answering it. We take it as referring to the light created in the first day, and pronounced by God to be good; and we will not believe that what has been pronounced good by Omnipotence, has been, or ever will be, annihilated; this light therefore continues, and may hereafter be developed on a far greater scale of magnificence than before, when there shall be no need of the sun, nor moon. But where is it now? and how is it hidden? are inquiries with which we are at once met, and in answer to which we beg to offer a few suggestions.

The aurora borealis has ever been the subject of great interest, and it is to this we attribute the primeval light, which doubtless has been allowed by the Omnipotent Creator to relapse from its former condition of resplendency into the dim obscurity which now pervades it. At times, however, it is subject to greater brilliancy, as the following account, given by Mr. E. J. Lowe, of the appearance of the aurora on the 9th March, 1861, as seen from the Beeston Observatory, will show.

"The aurora borealis of this evening has not been surpassed in magnificence and brilliancy for some years. The milk-white arch was delicately beautiful beyond description. In 1841, on the 22nd March, Professor Phillips, at York, and Professor Stevelly, at Belfast, saw a similar arch, and one less beautiful was seen at the Highfield House, on the

3rd December, 1845. Throughout the evening there was an auroral glare, which increased in intensity until from nine till eleven, p.m. The sky was a blaze of various coloured beams, coruscations, and arches. There was a low arch in the north, a red arch reaching to the altitude of Polaris, and a colourless arch south of the zenith. It was a broad band of soft, calm, strong, steady, dazzling, white light, broadest at the apex, and apparently rolling round upon itself with great rapidity, with a short, tremulous, vibratory, and undulatory motion." Doubtless, could we but penetrate the icy regions of the north, and enter into the treasures of the snow, we should there behold some of the most striking displays of Omnipotent skill and wisdom. We have repeatedly heard it remarked by men of the greatest scientific attainments, that it is in the highest degree probable that the aurora borealis is the germ of a band or flood of light, which at some distant period may encircle the world. We take an opposite view of the case by supposing that to be the original condition of it, and that it has subsided to its present limits. Moreover, the light produced by any electrical phenomena would be such as was best suited to the requirements of the period of which we write; the light would have been unaccompanied by heat, and as the earth at this time possessed innately a superabundance of warmth, it did not require any, as we do now, from exterior causes.

Thus, then, or from some similar cause, are we to suppose that light was produced on the first day.

We must say, the view taken by some writers, respecting the introduction of light on the first day, is anything but a satisfactory one; we mean, the supposition that the light was produced by the partial clearing away of the mists and clouds which loaded the atmosphere in this comparatively early age of the earth (the result of its still heated condition), and by this means allow the light *from the sun* to disseminate its rays over the surface of the earth, with a kind of suffused illumination or twilight, but not sufficient to allow of the sun being visible; and yet the light was pronounced by the Creator as being good. But this is not the principal objection we have to this theory; indeed, we cannot countenance any theory which invests the sun with light previous to the fourth day.

The second day was confined to the creation of the firmament, and the dividing of the waters; but, doubtless, the time occupied was as great as on the first or any succeeding day.

Genesis i. 6 to 8.—" And God said, Let there be a firmament in the midst of the waters, and

D

let it divide the waters from the waters. And God made the firmament, and divided the waters which were under the firmament from the waters which were above the firmament: and it was so. And God called the firmament Heaven. And the evening and the morning were the second day."

We regard the work of God on this day as being of more difficult explanation than any other. No science casts one shade of light upon it—rather the reverse; but we feel disposed to attach much greater significance to it than most people. The mere division of the water in the clouds from the water beneath them—our seas and oceans—answers but very faintly to the Mosaic account; more especially when we take into consideration the literal interpretation of the passage from the Hebrew, which would seem to intimate a solidity of the firmament (*rakia*), something beaten or spread out. There is, in fact, we feel assured, something altogether faulty in our knowledge of the subject, and on which we would not even venture to offer any explanation. Nor do certain passages of Scripture, referring to this subject, throw any light upon it. In the Psalms we read of the " waters that be above the heavens;"* in Job, that " the waters are

* Psalm cxlviii. 4.

hid as with a stone, and the face of the deep is frozen;"* and in Jeremiah, "He hath stretched out the heavens by His discretion, when He uttereth His voice, there is a multitude of waters in the heavens."†

We shall not enter into any further detail respecting the second day's creation, further than to state that it was during this time that the various slate strata and other primary rocks were being formed.

These rocks are entirely destitute of fossiliferous remains, either animal or vegetable, and therefore up to this period all was barren and lifeless. It is probable, however, that some of the silurian, or lower transition rocks, were formed about this period, and in which are found certain organic fossilized remains, which have induced geologists to attribute to this age the first dawn of animal life. By some this statement may be supposed not to be in accordance with Scripture, but a careful study of the subject will convince otherwise.

If you refer to the creation on the fifth day, you read that God said, " Let the waters bring forth abundantly the moving creature that *hath* life; " which would signify that they existed before, but in less numbers; and there can be little doubt that soon after the creation

* Job xxxviii. 30.   † Jeremiah x. 12, 13.

of light, certain lower kinds of life were developed.

The third day's creation seems to have been divided into two distinct parts: first, the gathering together of the waters, and the appearance of dry land; and second, the creation of the various trees, herbs, and other vegetation.

Genesis i. 9 to 13.—"And God said, Let the waters under the heaven be gathered together unto one place, and let the dry land appear: and it was so. And God called the dry land Earth; and the gathering together of the waters called He Seas: and God saw that it was good. And God said, Let the earth bring forth grass, the herb yielding seed, and the fruit-tree yielding fruit after his kind, whose seed is in itself upon the earth: and it was so. And the earth brought forth grass, and herb yielding seed after his kind, and the tree yielding fruit, whose seed was in itself, after his kind: and God saw that it was good. And the evening and the morning were the third day."

Perhaps it would be more proper to regard the first part of the third day as set apart for the preparation of the world, for the creation of the trees, &c., rather than to regard it as a division of creation; inasmuch as it required no creative power to call forth the land from the waters, but merely an exercise of power over the things which had been created.

First, then, we have to consider the probable means which were employed for raising the submerged earth from beneath the waters. And we must suppose now that we have arrived at a time, geologically speaking, of the completion of the Devonian system, or upper system of the lower transition rocks, and immediately preceding the upper transition, or carboniferous system.

At this period it is pretty nearly agreed by all geologists that a great upheaval took place; and we therefore regard the appearance of dry land at this time as arising from the throwing up of the superincumbent strata, by the accumulated subterranean forces, and the gathering together of the waters as a natural consequence. The description given of the former part of this day coincides with these mighty changes. To such changes and upheavals the earth has been more or less subjected ever since, manifestations of which are seen in every direction on the earth's surface; and from causes such as these was the command of God obeyed for the dry land to appear, and the waters to be gathered together.

We have now, in the second place, to consider the creation which followed, viz., vegetation. Now, we can readily suppose, that after such a convulsion as we have just been describing, great heat would have been liberated; and it was doubtless during this more than tropical warmth that the various trees and ferns which form our coal strata were developed." Coal is nothing else than compressed masses of vegetable matter, which, under the continued pressure of enormous weight, and an incalculable lapse of ages, has taken the consistency, colour, and properties with which we are so familiar. The vegetation must, indeed, have been luxuriant and extensive, far beyond what in modern times we have any example, even in the most fertile savannahs of India and America. Were the mighty forests of America laid low by one terrible catastrophe, and converted into coal, they would not, we are assured, be found enough for the production of a mere fraction of that mass of this material which exists beneath the surface of that continent.*

Wonderful as these statements appear, yet they are nevertheless true; and it is more than probable that such trees as we are in the habit of seeing could not have existed at all at this period.

The great warmth produced from the up-

* Pre-Adamite Man, p. 73.

heaval of the earth, whose surface was still only partially cooled, together with the moist and humid condition of the atmosphere, favoured the production of trees, which, although of gigantic magnitude, possessed but few of the characteristics of the trees of the present dispensation; trees, whose prodigious stems, rather than trunks, were of such speedy development, that the wood, if such it could be called, must have been excessively soft and pithy, and in no way resembling the wood of our hard, sturdy, and slow-growing trees. Ferns, reeds, and grasses, too, existed, whose size seems to us to be altogether fabulous; and it is to this immense vegetation of the third day that we owe the enormous extent and productiveness of our coal-measures, and which at the grand crisis of the world may fulfil an important office (in the hands of the Creator) in its destruction.

This brings us to the consideration of the fourth day.

Genesis i. 14 to 19.—"And God said, Let there be lights in the firmament of heaven to divide the day from the night; and let them be for signs, and for seasons, and for days, and years: and let them be for lights in the firmament of the heaven, to give light upon the earth: and it was so. And God made two great

lights; the greater light to rule the day, and the
lesser light to rule the night: He made the
stars also. And God set them in the firmament of the heaven, to give light upon the
earth, and to rule over the day and over the
night, and to divide the light from the darkness: and God saw that it was good. And
the evening and the morning were the fourth
day."

We have already expressed our belief that
the sun and moon were created simultaneously
with the earth; and, furthermore, we see
nothing in the above account which would lead
us to suppose otherwise; it neither asserts,
nor in any way infers, that these bodies were
created on this day; and it might with perfect
propriety be understood to convey the idea of
investing those bodies—previously created—
with light.

In the 16th verse, it says, " God made two
lights;" and whatever question may arise from
the use of the word " create," there can none
occur here, for the use of the word " made"
must obviously mean to produce—to fashion
from something already existing; and as the
light must have been thus produced, from what
other source could it have originated excepting
from the body of the sun which it envelopes ?

That the incandescent solar atmosphere

must have taken an immense time for its formation, there can be little doubt; the mere fact of its occupying the whole of the fourth day will confirm this opinion; but as to the way it originated, or by what means it is replenished, it is not easy to offer any precise opinion, although it seems probable that it is composed of excessively attenuated particles of matter in the most intense state of incandescence (this opinion has been much strengthened from the recent discoveries in spectrum analysis), which may have been thrown off from the sun in a gaseous or volatile condition from intense heat.

The last clause of the 16th verse, "He made the stars also," we were formerly of opinion, was merely a simple statement of the fact of God having made the stars, without any indication as to the time they *were* made; and yet it seemed somewhat out of place so regarded. We are now more inclined to the opinion that it refers to the clothing of those bodies with light, which, although created contemporary with our sun in the beginning, were not invested with light until this fourth day; further, the sun and moon have been previously spoken of in the same verse as "two great lights," and therefore this reference to the stars may inversely mean the same.

There is every probability that during this time the third day's creation was being perfected, or, in other words, that vegetation then assumed a condition more suited to the requirements of the animal world, as this period corresponds to the formation of the magnesium limestone, and the new red sandstone series, which are those immediately following the deposition of the coal-measures, and which, although generally destitute of fossilized remains, exhibit traces of life perhaps equally interesting, in the shape of impressions or footprints on the sandstone of various birds and animals of different descriptions. " In these fossilized footsteps we see the actual imprints of the feet of the animals as they lived, and not merely the remains of their bones. In the States of Massachusetts and Connecticut, in North America, where the new red sandstone occupies a space 150 miles long, and from ten to fifteen miles broad, there have been discovered impressions of the feet of thirty-two species of bipeds and of twelve species of quadrupeds. From the immense size of some of these footprints, it appears that birds living at that period must have been much larger than any now existing. Some of the footprints of birds are four times larger than the foot of an ostrich, and equal in size to those of the dinornis, a gigantic bird, which at no distant period lived in Australia.

The most remarkable impressions of four-footed creatures, preserved in the new red sand-stone, are those of prodigious frogs; some of the prints of the hind feet being eight inches long and five inches broad, and of the fore feet, four inches by three. Impressions of the fore and hind feet occur two inches apart, and the separation of each pair of footsteps is fourteen inches."*

We trust that we shall not be misunderstood here, for although we have unmistakeable proof of these animals existing before the time of their specified creation, still their numbers may have been so limited as to be unworthy of notice, until the command of God went forth that they should be brought forth abundantly.

The account given in Genesis of the fifth day, now under consideration, would seem, as we have before mentioned, to intimate in the most forcible manner that such was the case.

Genesis i. 20 to 23.—"And God said, Let the waters bring forth abundantly the moving crea-ture that hath life, and fowl that may fly above the earth in the open firmament of heaven. And

* Bakewell's "Illustrated Geology," p. 41.

God created great whales, and every living
creature that moveth, which the waters brought
forth abundantly, after their kind, and every
winged fowl after his kind : and God saw that
it was good. And God blessed them, saying,
Be fruitful, and multiply, and fill the waters
in the seas, and let fowl multiply in the earth.
And the evening and the morning were the
fifth day."

The very expression, " bring forth abundantly," would imply that such creatures did
previously exist. And, doubtless, the whole of
this, the fifth day, was set apart for the progressive development of those creatures. The
abundance of reptilian fossils in lias, the
lowest formation of the middle secondary
strata, would seem to point out this, the oolitic
system, as analogous to the fifth day's creation.
" In the times of the oolite," says Miller, " the
reptilian class dominated everywhere, and
possessed itself of all the elements. Gigantic
enaliosaurus, huge reptilian whales mounted
on paddles, were the tyrants of the ocean, and
must have reigned supreme over the already
reduced class of fishes. Pterodactyles, dragons,
as strange as ever were feigned by romances
of the middle ages, and that to the jaws and
teeth of the crocodile added the wings of a
bat, and the body and tail of an ordinary

mammal, had the 'power of the air,' and pursuing the fleetest insects in their flight, captured and bore them down. Some of these dragons of the secondary ages were of very considerable size. The wings of the pterodactyles of the chalk, in the possession of Mr. Bowerbank, must have had a spread of about eighteen feet; those of a recently discovered pterodactyle of the green sand, a spread of no less than twenty-seven feet. The lammer-geyer of the Alps, one of the largest existing European birds, has an extent of wing of but from ten to eleven feet; while that of the great condor of the Andes, the largest of flying birds of our own age, does not exceed twelve feet. The lakes and rivers of the oolitic period abounded in crocodiles and fresh-water tortoises of ancient type and fashion, and the woods and plains were the haunts of strange reptilian forms of what have been well termed 'fearfully great lizards,' some of which, such as the iguanodon, rivalled the largest elephant in height, and greatly more than rivalled him in length and bulk."

Many of these are well represented at the Crystal Palace Gardens, at Sydenham, and such were the occupants of the earth on the fifth day.

The sixth day, as we might reasonably have

expected, commences with the introduction of a much higher order of creatures.

Genesis i. 24 to 31.—"And God said, Let the earth bring forth the living creature after his kind, cattle, and creeping thing, and beast of the earth after his kind: and it was so. And God made the beast of the earth after his kind, and cattle after their kind, and everything that creepeth upon the earth after his kind: and God saw that it was good. And God said, Let us make man in our image, after our likeness : and let them have dominion over the fish of the sea, and over the fowl of the air, and over the cattle, and over all the earth, and over every creeping thing that creepeth upon the earth. So God created man in His own image, in the image of God created He him ; male and female created He them. And God blessed them, and God said unto them, Be fruitful, and multiply, and replenish the earth, and subdue it : and have dominion over the fish of the sea, and over the fowl of the air, and over every living thing that moveth upon the earth. And God said, Behold, I have given you every herb bearing seed, which is upon the face of all the earth, and every tree, in the which is the fruit of a tree yielding seed ; to you it shall be for meat. And to every beast of the earth, and to every fowl of the air, and to everything that creepeth upon the earth, wherein there is life, I have given every green herb for meat : and it was so. And God saw everything that He had made, and, behold, it was very good. And the evening and the morning were the sixth day."

The foregoing account is divided into two distinct parts. The first portion (verses 24 and 25) being set apart for the introduction of the cattle and beast of the earth; and the second portion (from verse 26 to 31) to man.

The cattle and beast of the earth, then, were all introduced in the early part of the sixth day; animals, which would be of the greatest service to man, and for which there had been no use previously, and there is no doubt that about this time the previous order of animals were fast becoming extinct, and, therefore, we are led to attribute to this period the formation of the wealdon and cretaceous, or chalk, systems. There has been a considerable amount of interest attaching itself to the formation of the wealdon beds, from the fact that although resting on rocks which must have been formed beneath the sea, they give unmistakeable evidence that they were formed above its level, and that afterwards they were again submerged; during which time the

various chalk beds were being formed. This
would indicate some great changes in the
condition of the globe.

The principal fossils discovered in chalk are
those of marine animals, fishes, and shells; and
although occasionally other remains have been
found, yet they are only sufficient to prove that
the whole surface of the earth, at this time, was
not covered with water; and the remains of
the animals so found must have been washed
out to sea, and thus preserved with the remains of the marine animals. We can readily
conceive, then, that during the deposition of
the chalk, the animal creation was going
through all its stages of progressive development, and at last it is completed. The earth
is clothed with verdure, and animals of elegant
form do sport and gambol beneath the out-
spreading branches of stately trees, whose ver-
dant tops, pointing upward, seemed to tell of
the glorious hand that made them. Bu tas
yet no prayerful voice is heard in thankfulness
ascending from this Eden, no one there possessed of intellect to appreciate the surrounding beauties. But, hark! the voice of the
Omnipotent Creator is again heard; the finish-
ing stroke is about to be given, and the top
stone is to be laid on the edifice. "And God
said, Let us make man in our own image, after

our likeness" (verse 26); and further, " So God created man in His own image, in the image of God created He him; male and female created He them" (verse 27); and having created them, immediately places them at the head of creation, and gives them dominion over all things, animate and inanimate.

Step by step we have been considering the various orders of creation; we have observed how the creation of one day has fitted and prepared the world for the next, and in what beautiful order one class of creatures has given place to others of a higher development and organization. We have watched with wondering admiration the infinite skill displayed by the Great Creator through the progressive ages, until at last we have seen the earth clothed in beauty, and fitted for the reception of the beings whom God, in His infinite wisdom, had ordained. And we have also seen how those beings were created in the image of God, and how all things were made subservient to their rule. In a future essay we shall have to consider who the occupants of the earth at this time were ? Whether they bore any reference to our first parent, Adam, or whether they must not be regarded as a distinct race of beings, whose existence on the earth must have been antecedent to Adam by an incalculably long

E

period.   Because, had Adam been created on
the sixth day, he must have lived throughout
the seventh or Sabbatic age—a period, we are
led to infer, of equal duration with either
of the six which preceded it; whereas we are
told that the extent of Adam's life was but nine
hundred and thirty years, which would be but
a mere fraction of the immensity of those
ages.

ESSAY III.

ON THE PROBABILITY OF THE EXISTENCE OF MAN BEFORE ADAM.

THE SABBATIC AGE—PRE-ADAMITE RACE—CREATION OF MAN; FIRST ACCOUNT—SECOND ACCOUNT—MAN'S DEPENDENCE—STONE IMPLEMENTS—THE ANGELS; THEIR ORIGIN AND EXISTENCE—ORIGIN OF SIN AND SATAN—ANGELS NOT IMMATERIAL BEINGS—WAR IN HEAVEN—THE GREAT UPHEAVAL—GLACIAL PERIOD—DESOLATION OF THE EARTH; ITS RESTITUTION.

WE have been so accustomed to regard Adam as the first occupant of our earth, that the proposition of a Pre-Adamite race having existed ages before him, might almost be expected to do great violence to people's feelings, and which has given rise to so much disputing and contention. But, however doubtful or improbable the idea may be thought, we nevertheless indulge in it ourselves; and trust, before the completion of this essay, to be enabled to show that it is neither so doubtful or improbable. On the contrary, we hope to be enabled to set

E 2

it forth in such a light that it shall be the
means of making clear the interpretation of
many perplexing passages of Scripture, and
which must ever remain so, unless we admit of
the existence of a Pre-Adamic race of beings.

In a previous essay we have shown that the
six days of creation, spoken of in Genesis, must
refer to immense periods of time; the deposition of the sedimentary rocks clearly prove that
they must have required ages upon ages in
their formation; and as the creation of each
successive day has left vestiges in the shape
of entombed and fossilized remains to identify
it with the rocks then forming, there can be no
doubt of the period—relatively, not chronologically speaking—of their formation.

Such being the case, we can come to no
other conclusion respecting the seventh day
than that it must have been of equal duration
to the six days which preceded it.

" The Sabbath was then an age. It was one
of divine and holy rest, during which, as it
rolled on, the calm and undisturbed blessedness resulting from God's approving smile
must have spread itself over all creation. With
ineffable complacency the Creator's eye sur-
veyed his newly peopled world, and man, the
last and brightest glory of the whole, attracted
the chief portion of his regard. No sin, no

sorrow, no evil, marred the perfection of the work; and having pronounced it "very good," this was the season when he rejoiced over its unsullied excellence, as yet unmarred by any form of ill."* Now, if we suppose that Adam is identified with the man here referred to, we must claim for him an age which Scripture distinctly asserts he never attained. For we read (Genesis v. 5), "And all the days that Adam lived were nine hundred and thirty years: and he died." Whereas, if the above supposition were true, we should have to count his age by hundreds of thousands of years, rather than mere hundreds. This, however, is but one argument in favour of a Pre-Adamite race; but we hope to prove still more clearly that the man spoken of in the first chapter of Genesis bore no reference to Adam.

Hugh Miller, writing on this subject, but leaving the possibility of a Pre-Adamite race altogether out of the question, attempts to overcome the difficulty respecting the length of the Sabbatic age, by supposing that Adam was created at the very end of the sixth day, and that the seventh is not yet completed, and that we are now passing through the Sabbatic age. He thus somewhat poetically describes it :—

"At length, as the day wanes, and the

* Pre-Adamite Man.

shadows lengthen, man, the responsible soul of creation, formed in God's own image, is introduced upon the scene, and the work of creation ceases for ever upon the earth; the night falls once more upon the prospect, and there dawns yet another morrow, the morrow of God's rest, that divine Sabbath in which there is no more creative labour, and which, blessed and sanctified beyond all the days that had gone before, has for its especial object the moral elevation and final redemption of man."*

At first sight there seems to be a certain amount of plausibility in it, but it will not bear investigation; what is there, we ask, in the present age, that partakes of a Sabbatic character?

" Could anything be less like the blessedness and stillness of the Sabbath rest, than the events which have ceaselessly followed, marking the grand eras of the history of man? . . . . The age was ushered in by his fall—an event which shook the moral universe to its centre. From this terrible catastrophe has issued an interminable series of obstinate struggles against God, and of murderous warfare among men.

" It was violence—of which the first example was given at the gate of Eden, by the first-born of our race—which, increasing till it became intolerable, brought on ungodly man

* On the Testimony of the Rocks, page 190.

the all but total destruction of a deluge.   It
was the spirit of ambition and rebellion, which
soon after rearing its proud towers on the plain
of Shinar, caused their dispersion.   It was
their wayward, wilful idolatry, and hatred of
God's government, that led to the call of
Abraham and his family as a peculiar people,
and the virtual excommunication of the rest of
the world, between whom and God a stern and
fatal controversy from that time forth ceased
not to rage.   It was the disloyalty and rebellion of this chosen family which caused
them, favoured though in many respects they
were, to be visited by prophets and angels, com-
missioned to teach, to remonstrate, and to warn
them of the divine anger, and at length to be
driven as exiles to Babylon ; nay, to be. ultimately dispersed, with indignation and terrible
judgments, to the four quarters of the world.
And since that era of judgment, the annals of
mankind have been chiefly marked by rebellion
against their Maker. . . . . .

" The very life of the Christian, as if in
unison with the unsettled character of the age,
is represented as a warfare; while, more than
all, the Son of God himself has proved the
passing age to be no Sabbath.   He has visited
our earth, but it was not to sway the sceptre
of a peaceful Sabbatic empire.   It was to enter

into stern conflict with the powers of darkness, and to rescue, by His agony and death, the people whom He loved, from the jaws of the destroyer." *

What, then—we feel constrained again to ask —is there in the passing age that would lead us to ascribe to it a Sabbatic character? But what says Scripture on this subject? Read the first three verses of the second chapter of Genesis, and there see what it says concerning it.

Genesis ii. 1 to 3.—" Thus the heavens and the earth were finished, and all the host of them. And on the seventh day God ended His work which He had made ; and He rested on the seventh day from all His work which He had made. And God blessed the seventh day, and sanctified it : because that in it He had rested from all his work which God created and made."

Here you see the seventh day is plainly spoken of as having passed, and no other rendering than this must be attempted. And thus are we induced to believe that the creation of man on the sixth day bore no reference to Adam. Without admitting the possibility of a Pre-Adamite race, certain passages of Scripture relating to creation become not only inexplicable, but actually antagonistic. See " Essays and Reviews : Mosaic Cosmogony."

* Pre-Adamite Man, p. 117.

It is owing to this fact, that many eminent writers, not taking into consideration the probability of the existence of a Pre-Adamite race, have confused the interpretation of such passages, and, we regret to say, have made anything but a praiseworthy use of them.

For instance, take the first and second chapters of the Book of Genesis, and we shall there find two separate and distinct accounts given of the creation of man, or rather creation on the one hand, and formation on the other, and each of these accounts differing considerably from one another. In the first chapter, man is described as being created; in the second, he is said to have been formed of the dust of the ground.

In the first chapter he is described as being created *after* the lower animals, and in the second he is made *first*, and the lower animals *after* him.

The first chapter speaks of male and female being created together, but in the account given in the second chapter, Adam is first formed, and existed alone for some time, ere Eve was taken from his side, the interval between the two being occupied by the planting of Eden and the formation of the animals, for it must be remembered that it was not until after Adam had named the various creatures which were brought to him, that God caused a deep sleep to fall on Adam. How long a time was thus occupied we are not told, but, doubtless, considerable time must have elapsed. The trees which formed the garden of Eden would occupy some time in growing to perfection, while the animals, we imagine, would not have been produced in an instant.

Thus it is evident, for a very long interval, Adam existed as the sole occupier of the earth; and there can be no doubt, arguing from Scripture, that when Adam was introduced, the earth, at that time, was little better than a barren waste; at least, so we are led to infer from the account given in the second chapter of Genesis. This barren condition of the earth is clearly indicated at the fifth verse, which reads thus : " And every plant of the field before it was in the earth, and every herb of the field before it grew ; for the Lord God had not caused it to rain upon the earth, and there was not a man to till the ground." And at this juncture God forms Adam from the dust of the ground, and *afterwards* brings forth the various things for his use. It would appear as though God would thus make Adam to feel his entire dependence on his Creator. How different does this appear when placed side by side with the account given of the creation of man on the sixth day. There he is made to enter a world clothed in beauty, and to have dominion over all the earth; not to enter a wilderness, or to be confined in a garden. He is to have entire dominion over *all* the earth, and everything animate or inanimate upon it; he is to be subject to no restrictions whatever—all things are placed in subjection under him; and, furthermore, to rejoice in the companionship of beings like himself, with whom he will be able to share with holy affection and admiration the glory, dominion, and power which God in His infinite majesty had been pleased to confer upon him.

Far different is it with Adam, however; called into a world despoiled of its beauty, and made to feel his littleness and dependence, he is ultimately placed in the garden of Eden—which, however beautiful it may have been, was, nevertheless, restricted in its limits—to dress and keep it. Afterwards, we find the animals are formed and brought unto Adam to receive their names, but we read of no dominion being given him over either them or the earth, although, doubtless, sufficient command was given for their subjugation to his service; however, the greatest restriction was that which involved his fall. He was warned, with a threat, not to partake of the fruit of a tree, " For," said God, " in the day that thou eatest thereof thou shalt surely die." How did he keep this command? He partook of the fruit, and with the result we are too well acquainted.

It is not necessary, however, that we should confine our remarks to the creation of man; there are various other passages in these two accounts of creation which do anything but agree, and would almost induce us to regard them, apart from anything else, as referring to entirely different events, as a careful study of the first two chapters in Genesis will show; and we have again to repeat, that without admitting the possibility of a Pre-Adamite race, these two chapters become not only inexplicable but actually antagonistic. We are, therefore, almost forced to the conclusion that these two accounts refer to two distinct and separate creations, differing in many respects widely from each other; and furthermore, that the creation of man on the sixth day bore no reference whatever to our first parent—Adam. And after making these broad statements, we are led into the inquiry as to the nature of the beings whom we choose to call Pre-Adamite, and who were called into being on the sixth day.

If we suppose the Pre-Adamite race to have been beings similar to ourselves, and endowed with like capacities, as it is very probable they were, might we not have expected to have discovered traces of their existence among the different strata which were being formed during their occupation of the earth?

"Now, if it were necessary to believe that the Pre-Adamite must have lived in cities similar to ours, that extensive buildings of stone were necessary to his happiness, and that his ambition or his pride must have imposed on him the task of rearing monuments enduring as brass, there might be reason in demanding some material proofs of his occupation—the foundations of some Babylon or Rome, for example; the capitals or plinths of some Colosseum or Parthenon, some Palmyra or Thebes, however ruinous. But the conditions of the Pre-Adamite imposed no necessity of this kind. His works needed no element of permanency in order to fulfil their purpose. Ambition, which belongs to fallen creatures, prompted him to the erection of no proud monuments of power or conquest. The necessities of the body were supplied almost spontaneously by the prolific soil on which he walked, and over which he ruled. His world, still warmed by its internal heat, and as yet uncursed by sin,

produced its perpetual harvests with amazing
prodigality.   Even much later, when God
placed Adam in Eden, all that he required was
poured into his bosom without toil.   And, as
in Eden Adam needed not to build houses for
his shelter, as he reared no mighty fabrics for
his support or his convenience, so must it have
been during the sinless reign of the former
race.   The Pre-Adamite had a wider domain
and a freer life than Adam in his Eden garden,
but we are to suppose that, unfallen like him,
his means of sustenance and of enjoyment were
as complete.   Both lived on the bounty of
their Divine Creator; the curse of labour had
fallen upon neither; the skies shed a genial
influence over them both; and no fervid heats
of summer, or chilly blasts of winter, imposed
the need of artificial shelter.   Even the distinctions of climate seem to have been unknown
at the earlier era of which we speak; and those
appliances to which men now so gladly resort,
to screen their bodies from surrounding influences, were not required.   He lived amid the
bounties of his Maker, content with the shelter
of umbrageous foliage or overhanging rocks. A
worshipper rather than a worker, he honoured
God by praise and lofty meditation rather than
by labour or service.   Unsinning, like Adam,
his life, like his, was of a kind unfavourable to

the bequest of enduring memorials to future ages; and as well might we now expect to find in the ancient Paradise the vestiges of its occupation by our first father, as to find in the scenes once peopled by a Pre-Adamic race, the marks and tokens of their existence." *

It is true, indeed, that certain rude stone implements have been discovered in various parts of the world, embedded in the upper tertiary deposits; even in England they have been found in great numbers, and in France still more so. The question which arises is, of what use could these rude instruments be to a people, under the circumstances we have just been speaking of? The only use which seems probable to us, would be for the tilling of the ground—if, indeed, it required it; or for subduing or repressing the lower animals, according to the command of God. These, during a time of rebellion, might have been used as implements of warfare, and others may have been made more adapted to such purposes. What ground there is for supposing such, will be considered further on.

Side-by-side with the question, who and what was the Pre-Adamite? we place another, viz., who and what are the angels, and whence their origin? We place these two questions

* Pre-Adamite Man, p. 137.

thus, as we believe in answering the one we have found the answer to the other—or, in other words, the angels and this Pre-Adamite race are but one and the same, and we shall now endeavour to explain our reasons for thinking so.

In the first place, if we recognise the angels as the race of beings created on the sixth day, and living in holiness and purity throughout the seventh or Sabbatic age, it gives an extra sublimity to the whole of creation. We see then how the beginning, spoken of in Genesis, was, in the highest sense of the word, *the beginning*, not even the angels before it. They, indeed, came and crowned the work of the creation; and then, in holy rest, the Almighty surveys His finished work throughout the long ages of the Sabbatic era, worshipped and adored by this angel host. Does not the Bible lead us to believe that the angels—all of them, both Satan and his followers, and those who kept their first estate—were all originally created in a holy and happy state? Our Lord, speaking of Satan, says, " He was a murderer from the beginning, and abode not in the truth " (John viii. 44); signifying that he was once identified with it.

Now let us suppose the Sabbatic era to be drawing to a close—that the ages of happiness and glory have rolled along. A spirit of rebellion is manifest, and Satan would attempt to wrest the government from the hands of the Almighty. His fall and humiliation are thus beautifully described:—

Isaiah xiv. 12 to 15.—" How art thou fallen from heaven, O Lucifer, Son of the Morning! how art thou cast down to the ground which didst weaken the nations! For thou hast said in thine heart, I will ascend into heaven; I will exalt my throne above the stars of God; I will sit also upon the mount of the congregation, in the sides of the north; I will ascend above the heights of the clouds; I will be like the Most High. Yet thou shalt be brought down to hell, to the sides of the pit."

We learn from the 12th verse of this passage, that Satan held at one time a high and exalted position among some beings; he is termed " Son of the Morning," and the beings referred to are represented as nations, which would seem to point to the earth as their abode, although in the first clause of the verse it is described as heaven; but the word heaven here may be simply descriptive of the heavenly beauty and perfection of the earth before he fell. In the succeeding verse, we read of another heaven spoken of, to which his ambition aspired; and this, we think, refers to the

heavenly abode of the Most High.   And there
is no reason why the earth, in its pristine
beauty and holiness, should not be termed
heaven—if, indeed, it did not form part of it.

If, therefore, by these means we identify the
angelic host as the Pre-Adamite race, who
occupied the earth during the Sabbatic age,
we must endeavour to glean from Scripture all
we can concerning them, their history, and
final removal.   In the first place, then, what
do we know concerning the angels?

We are aware that, by the vast majority of
people, the angels are considered as immaterial and spiritual beings—and this belief we
are warranted from Scripture in saying is altogether erroneous and untrue.   If it were not
so, there is an end at once to the supposition
of their having inhabited the earth ; as immaterial beings, they would not have required a
material world for their abode.   Let us not be
misunderstood here : we do not say the angels
are not spiritual beings—all we say is, that
they are not immaterial, but that they are
possessed of glorified bodies, and therefore
capable of enjoying, in common with ourselves,
all things pertaining to a material universe ;
and were it not that we know how strongly
prejudiced the popular mind is on this subject,
we might almost have deemed it unnecessary

to have quoted Scripture in support of our views; as it is, we shall invite your attention while we quote a few from the many passages of Scripture which not only favour this belief, but will admit of no other.

Take, for instance, the account given in Genesis xviii., and there read how Abraham entertains the three angels who appear before him as he is seated within the door of the tent; he runs out to meet them, and after bowing himself before them, he invites them to stay. He says, " Let a little water, I pray you, be fetched, and wash your feet, and rest yourselves under the tree." Now, who ever heard of washing a spirit's feet, or of a spirit's resting? But, more than this, we find Abraham immediately afterwards busily engaged in preparing a meal for them.

Genesis xviii. 6 to 8.—"And Abraham hastened into the tent unto Sarah, and said, Make ready quickly three measures of fine meal, knead it, and make cakes upon the hearth. And Abraham ran unto the herd, and fetched a calf, tender and good, and gave it unto a young man, and he hasted to dress it. And he took butter, and milk, and the calf which he had dressed, and set it before them ; and he stood by them under the tree, and they did eat." They partook of the food thus provided; they did not disdain this human fare ; *and they did eat.* And from this we learn that they must have been something more than mere spirits."

In the 19th chapter we find the same angels appearing to Lot ; and after great pressing on his part, he prevails on them to stay the night with him, " and he made them a feast, and did bake unleavened bread, and they did eat."

We learn also from this chapter that their appearance was as men, for as such they were spoken of by the people of Sodom. And in the morning we find them using physical force, and thus compelling Lot and his wife and daughters to leave the doomed city. And we consider this as the greatest and most conclusive evidence of the material existence of the angels. In the 78th Psalm there is a reference made to the children of Israel, during their sojourn in the wilderness, partaking of angels' food. " Man did eat angels' food : he sent them meat to the full."—(Psalm lxxviii. 55.) From this we are led to infer that the angels partake of nourishment as well as men, and that nourishment must be for the support of a material body.

The Bible abounds with instances of the appearance of angels ; and almost in every case do they show forth their material as well as their spiritual nature. Even the fact of their being able to converse with men, is sufficient to prove them possessed of a corporeal nature.

We shall quote another instance of the appearance and conversation of angels with men, or rather, in this instance, with women. We refer to the appearance of the two angels to the Galilean women at the sepulchre.

Luke xxiv. 4 to 6.—" And it came to pass, as they were much perplexed thereabout, behold *two men* stood by them in shining garments. And as they were afraid, and bowed down their faces to the earth, they said unto them, Why seek ye the living among the dead ? He is not here, but is risen."

. The angels in this passage are spoken of as men; " *two men* stood by them in shining garments," which would indicate the human aspect they wore. Their language was human; and the sympathy which they evinced to those wondering and anxious women would indicate also that, albeit they *were* angels, yet they possessed a corporeal and earthly character; and in this respect, at least, will meet the requirements of a Pre-Adamite race. In the second place, having established their identity with the Pre-Adamite, we are led to inquire as to the nature and history of their existence on the earth ?

If we turn to geology for an answer, we find

it speechless. The testimony of the rocks bears no testimony of their existence or history, for beyond the rough-hewn implements we have before considered, there is nothing which we could suppose to bear any reference to them. Nature is silent, and the earth holds the secrets in oblivion. The sun and moon shone then as now, but they cast not one ray of light to illumine the dark obscurity in which their existence is wrapped. The *silent* stars which deck our skies were subject to their admiration, and they, too, merit the title given them. We breathe the air they breathed; but the tale is still untold. Where, then, shall we look, or from whence shall our answer come?

We turn once again to Scripture, and we find that after their creation there is a command given; they are to " replenish the earth and subdue it;" and to do this effectually, dominion is given them over the earth, and all things pertaining to it. Now, for the word replenish might be read to fill— to consummate, to complete; and doubtless their existence was spent in carrying out this command, and thus was the seventh day spent. And we find that the Hebrew for " seven" comes from a root signifying " to be full, complete, entirely made up," and thus beautifully describes the condition to which the world had then arrived.

They were to subdue the earth; and this doubtless meant that they were to repress the undue extension of the lower animals, for which purpose the so-called implements of warfare may have been used.

We have now, in the third and last place, to consider the circumstance which brought about their removal.

We read (Rev. xii. 7, &c.): "There was war in heaven: Michael and his angels fought against the dragon, and the dragon fought and his angels, and prevailed not; neither was their place found any more in heaven." The heaven spoken of here we regard as another instance where the earth, in its original glory, is spoken of as heaven. And it is here we find the origin of sin and Satan. For ages had the great deceiver lived and occupied an exalted position among this heavenly host; he was there "when the morning stars sang together, and all the sons of God shouted for joy" (Job xxxviii. 7); and his ambition now prompted him to go higher. He had power, and he knew it; and he found those who sided with him. Sin entered, and the war commenced and raged with unabated fury, and the once beautiful earth becomes a field of carnage; it heaves and swells; the mountain sides gush forth with fire, and darken with their fumes the mid-day

sun ; wild hurricanes lash the oceans into
fury ; the thunder rolls with deafening peals,
and the fierce lightning in swift succession
rends the stately trees ; at length a deafening
crash is heard, and the remnants of its beauty
are hurried into complete destruction. "Michael
and his angels fought against the dragon," they
obtained the victory, and ascended up to
heaven. "The dragon fought, and his angels,
and prevailed not," and was cast out. And
thus were they removed, leaving behind them,
in the place of all that was beautiful, a wreck
which, even to the present day, is everywhere
apparent.   The testimony of all geologists
agree that from the lower strata upwards there
are indications of a steady progress, up to a
point where the organisms have reached their
highest development and perfection ; and that
at this point striking proofs are everywhere
manifest of a wide-spread and universal catastrophe, which must have swept over the world,
and converted its then glorious surface into
utter desolation and destruction.   " These
must have originated in the action of elemental
powers, whose force and universality it is impossible to exaggerate.   They are confined to
no locality.   The mountain stream wears its
way to the lowlands through banks of this
débris.   The railway-cutting brings it to light

in the plains.   Wherever nature or art lays open the superficial deposits, the fact is demonstrated that clay, mingled with worn stones, scratched and striated, has been forced forward through an agency of inconceivable power, and laid in masses, often of enormous thickness, over the earlier surface.   Alluvial deposits, which must have owed their origin to causes belonging to the same period, but deriving their peculiar features from lakes and rivers, are found in many parts of Europe.   They are seen in the valleys of the Rhine, the Rhone, and other great rivers ; on the great plain of Craw, in the south of France, having an extent of fifty square leagues ; on the plain of Bavaria, and that which spreads itself out at the foot of the Alps over the states of Lombardy and Venice." *

" Over all the rocks of the tertiary era, and painfully contrasting with the proofs they enclose of flowers once beautiful, and fruitful plants, and noble animals, the relics of races which flourished ere they became indurated, and which must therefore have graced, as we believe, the sixth and seventh Mosaic ages, and over the rocks of every other description which at that time were superficial, are to be seen by the most unpractised eye the

* Lardner's " Popular Geology," sect. 554.

remains and evidences of this complete ruin.
The clay of our wheat countries, the till of less
fertile soils, the gravel and sand of our barren
commons, the huge stones and scattered
boulders that disfigure the sides of our mountain vales, and lie in hideous confusion on
many an upland that faces and confronts the
opening of rapidly descending valleys, together
with the scratched and abraded surfaces of the
rocks and of the rolled stones in all such loca-
lities, everywhere tell the same tale, and teach
the same dread lesson. . . . It is a most
curious inquiry, What were the causes of a convulsion capable of producing these strange and
terrible effects? Many overturns and fiery
revolutions the world must doubtless have previously undergone, but there are marks of a
judicial and penal character in this, which are
to be found in none of these. It came when
the world was complete; when its fauna and
its flora were perfect. It came after the productions of the Creator's hand were pronounced
not only '*good*,' but '*very good*.' This utter
extinction of animal and vegetable life at its
very prime has in it a primitive character, such
as does not belong to the fiery throes of the
earlier convulsions; and to whatever elemental
agencies the ruin is to be traced, the results
will not contradict the conclusion that they

must have originated in the just displeasure of the offended Creator."*

We have now to see what followed. The first occupants of the earth are removed, and it is left for a time to desolation; a desolation which may bear its traces to eternity as a testimony of the consequences of sin, and the manifestation of God's just and righteous indignation.

It has been supposed that these immense changes and upheavals were followed by what is termed the Glacial Period, which divided the diluvial from the present; a period during which it is supposed the earth was invested with an almost universal covering of ice, and from which it is presumed may be accounted the preservation of some of the existing flora of the diluvial period, the seeds of which, being preserved in the ice until the time of its dissolution, when they would spring up with the returning warmth and flourish and grow. And in the same manner may have been preserved various ova of insects, butterflies, &c., &c., which have been proved by experiment to sustain no injury from the severest cold which has ever been produced by artificial agency, which, we scarcely need remark, greatly exceeds any cold that exists naturally. Dr. Hunter

* Pre-Adamite Man.

gives an account of his having submitted
the ova of various insects and moths to a
cold 22° below zero; and from which, nevertheless, caterpillars came from all the eggs,
and that, too, contemporary with others which
had not been subjected to the cold.

Dr. Lardner, in an article of the *Edinburgh
New Philosophical Journal,* writing on the period
referred to above, says :—

" It is this period of our earth, to inquire
into the existence of which, and its entrench-
ment upon our present epoch, I have long
assigned myself, as a problem whose existence
the men of science, at first, would not even
give themselves the trouble to deny, till the
force of truth obtained the triumph over many,
if not over all, and constrained a recognition
of the justness of what used to produce only a
compassionate smile, as the lamentable aber-
ration of an over-strained fancy.

" This *glacial period* is the epoch of separation betwixt the diluvial period, as it has been
termed by geologists, and our present period;
it is it which, like a sharp sword, has separated
the totality of now living organisms from their
predecessors, which lie interred in the sands of
our plains, or below the ice of our polar
regions. Lastly, it is it which has left to our
times the testimonies of its former greatness,

upon the tops and in the valleys of our Alps. . . . .

"I have followed the marks along the coasts of England, Scotland, and Ireland; and no doubt can now be raised in regard to the fact, that in our latitude the ice extended to below the level of the present sea. At many points of these coasts I have, as far as my eye could penetrate the water, seen these traces deep below the surface; and so indelible are they, so deeply imprinted are these characteristic marks, that the rising breakers have not even yet been able to erase them."

If all these facts, then, be true—as doubtless they are—to what a desolation the earth must have been reduced, how painfully would it compare with its previous magnificence and glory; robbed of its stately trees, which may have been swept from its surface by one chill, icy blast; divested of its inhabitants and devastated of its beauty by one dread tumultuous catastrophe, it left behind a desolation which must have been sublimely and awfully grand, from its worse than death-like stillness. But God in His infinite wisdom had not willed it to remain so; for the time at length arrives for the renewed display of the Great Creator's power, and it was this renewal that ushered in the present dispensation, and to which the account given in the second chapter of Genesis must alone refer. It was then our first parent, Adam, was formed from the dust of the ground. How different his position to the men who preceded him! how much more humble and lowly his origin than theirs! Formed from the dust on which he treads, he boasts not of their noble origin. They were under no restraint; dominion was given them over all the earth, and all upon it; while he is confined to a garden to dress and keep it, and thus made to feel his dependence on his Creator; and even there is subjected to restrictions which eventually involve his fall, but which nevertheless —thanks be unto God in Christ Jesus—will ultimately result in placing him on the highest seat of glory, and even above those of our fore-runners, who kept their first estate. And we are led with the Psalmist to exclaim, " For thou hast made him a little lower than the angels, and hast crowned him with glory and honour."*

* An excellent work on this subject, entitled " Pre-Adamite Man," published by J. Nisbet & Co., and to which we have occasionally referred, will be found absorbingly interesting, as entering more fully into the detail than our prescribed limits would allow. It is a work we feel proud in recommending, and one which, we must admit, has given great tone to our opinions on this subject. It is worthy of remark, from the sterling piety which is manifested throughout by the writer.

ESSAY IV.

ON THE PHYSICAL CONSTITUTION OF THE UNIVERSE.

THE SCIENCES AND THEIR TEACHINGS—GEOLOGY—CHEMISTRY—ASTRONOMY—METEOROLOGY—METEORS : THEIR COMPOSITION—ELEMENTS OF THE ANCIENTS—FIRE NOT AN ELEMENT—WATER : COMBINATION OF TWO GASES—IRON AN ELEMENT—METALS AND METALLOIDS—OXYGEN : ITS COMBINATIONS—COMBINATION OF IRON—LIST OF ELEMENTARY SUBSTANCES.

WE have ever been prone to regard the various branches of science which engage the attention, and form the study of the contemplative minds of men, as *one* grand study, *one universal* science ; and we believe the title of our essay will comprehend all of them. And whatever may be either said or thought with reference to our opinions, we shall at least claim the merit of having selected a title broad enough ; one, indeed, which is capable of treating from the atomic particle, whose

infinitesimal dimensions are undiscernible to
the eye, even when assisted by the most powerful microscopic agency, to the huge planets
or gigantic suns which stretch far and wide
into infinitude.   Our only fear was, from the
vastness of the subject, that of not being able
to retain it within reasonable limits—for, truly,
it might well be considered illimitable.   And
although, at present, we must confine ourselves
more particularly to the primary, or, more properly, the elementary condition of the material
universe, still it will be interesting, and, we
think, not out of place, to glance over the
various ways, and to notice under what distinctions the *physical constitution of the universe*
is studied.

If we suppose the original condition of the
universe to have been that of excessively
attenuated particles of matter, there is an
interesting field open for inquiry, as to what
position the various elementary substances
occupied, relatively speaking, one to the other;
whether they existed in a confused chaotic
mass, or whether they were arranged in belts
or zones around the point of condensation,
according to their various densities or specific
gravities.   The latter would certainly appear
most probable ; for, unless such were the case,
it is almost impossible to conceive how the

various metals which are discovered in veins
could have so accumulated. And, besides
which, it seems more consistent with the
systematic order of the Creator's works, as
well as the teachings of philosophy. By some
it has been supposed that matter originally
was composed of one elementary body, and
that what we regard as the elementary substances are only modifications of this original
matter; we must avoid, however, any metaphysical inquiry. We cannot, of course, get
at the idea as to what matter *is* in the eyes of
God—whether it is composed of ultimate
elementary particles, which obey certain laws
of molecular attraction, and thus produce what
we term the elements; or whether it always
possessed the same distinctive qualities as it
does at present.

If we look around us, matter in every varied
form is presented to our view; and it is the
study of these various forms and configura-
tions, in one way or another, which has given
rise to the many different sciences with which
we are familiar. It is the work of the geologist to dig into the bowels of the earth, to
penetrate its caverns, and wander amidst its
rocky tenantry, and for what else but that he
may learn and bring to light their physical
development and constitution? It is the work

of the chemist to penetrate deeper into the mysteries thus revealed, and to resolve them into their constituent elements.   The work of the chemist, however, does not end here; for, beyond ascertaining the various combinations which exist naturally, and discovering the laws which govern them, he is enabled to make them assume new forms of an entirely different character.   He, too, joins with the astronomer in the contemplation of the heavenly bodies; and by the analysis of the light which streams from them, even from the distance of millions of millions of miles, he is enabled to link our earth and the solar system with the most remote of the fixed stars, and boldly to proclaim, not only that they are similarly constituted, but is also enabled to tell us how their light is produced, and from what combinations it arises.

The study of meteorology also adds its quota to our information.   The meteoric masses which are constantly falling to the surface of the earth, neither contain anything extraordinary, or much differing from that which belongs more directly to the earth. At present, no new substance has come to us from without.   The result of the most careful analysis of these bodies shows them on an average not to contain more than about twenty of the elementary substances which, up to the present time, have been discovered on the earth. They—most of them—present a very metallic appearance; and iron, the most abundant of our terrestrial metals, enters largely into their constitution, and in many instances to the extent of eighty to ninety per cent. of the entire mass. Tin, copper, and manganese are, generally, also found in greater or less quantities.

From all these facts, we are induced to regard the entire universe in the same way as we should contemplate the earth as a part of it, as that which refers to a part is common to the whole; and the same laws which govern the one also govern the other. It is the same hand that formed the earth that created the sun and the moon. " He made the stars also." And although we might reasonably expect to find great diversity of form, and manifestations of every varied description, yet each, we should imagine, would display on examination the same characteristics, and point to the singleness and uniformity of the work of the Allwise and Unchanging Creator. Thus, then, recognising matter as presented to us here, as indicative or representative of what matter is throughout the universe, we shall be enabled to start at once with the subject of its elementary character.

We look back on our school days with a smile, when we remember being taught that there are four elements, viz.—*fire, water, earth, and air*. Such, indeed, was the philosophy of the ancients; neither of these, however, are either elements, or partake of an elementary character. Fire is not an element, but is an effect produced by the union and disunion of various elements during combustion. Fire, indeed, is not a substance at all, but merely a condition which matter assumes in accordance with certain natural causes.

Water is not an element, but a compound body, produced by the union of two gases, oxygen and hydrogen, in the proportion of one volume of the former to two of the latter; this fact is very easily demonstrated, by first mixing the gases in these proportions in a strong glass vessel, and then applying a light; the result will be, they will enter into immediate combination one with another, and explode with violence, producing water, which will condense on the sides of the vessel in small globules. It would require three thousand gallons of these gases to produce one gallon of water.

It is a somewhat singular fact, that we never

light a fire, nor a candle, without the production of water, as a result; it is easily accounted
for, however, if we recollect that the very
elements which enter into the combination of
water are those which unite during combustion. Thus, if a piece of cold metal be held
over a flame, or even a fire, for a few seconds,
its surface will become coated with moisture,
arising from the union of the gases in combustion.

Earth is obviously not an element, as, of
course, it consists of all the elementary substances combined; and therefore nothing could
be more erroneous than this ancient supposition.

And, finally, the air is not an element,
although more nearly approaching it than the
others. It consists of four measures of nitrogen
gas, and one of oxygen, with small quantities of
carbonic acid, and water in a state of vapour.

And now, having done with the so-called
elements of the ancients, we turn our attention
to the consideration of what really constitutes
an elementary substance.

If we turn to the dictionary, we find that
elementary is described as meaning *uncom-
pounded*, having *only one principle;* we might
describe it as that which is incapable of de-
composition, and we think this will give a

pretty correct idea of what is meant by an element.

Thus, iron is found to be an element, because chemistry proves it to be a simple body, and from which, alone, no two substances can be produced; and therefore iron may be taken as a type of the solid elementary substances, while oxygen, which is also an element, will represent the characteristics of the gaseous elementary substances. We have but one example of a liquid element at the general temperature around us, and that is the metal mercury, or quicksilver; * although there can be little doubt that each and all of the solid elementary substances are capable of assuming either of the three conditions, solid, liquid, or gaseous; it is only a question of producing sufficient heat.

Up to the present time, chemistry has revealed to us no less than sixty-three of these elementary substances.

These elementary substances are divided into two classes—the metals, and the metalloids or non-metallic elements; and to one of these classes, or the other, must belong each and every simple body in the material creation. The former—the metals—are by far the more numerous, and comprise of course the whole

---

* Bromine is also liquid.

of the metallic bases; while the metalloids, although comparatively few in proportion, comprise the various gases, and those of the simple bodies which are found not to possess a metallic character.

Many of these substances are very rare, and seldom or ever used in chemical manipulations. Some, indeed, although known to exist, have defied all our efforts to reduce them to their simple or elementary forms; and others which *have* been so reduced, have such an affinity for and unite so quickly with oxygen, that even a limited exposure to atmospheric influences is sufficient to reinstate or recompose them to their original condition. The metals potassium and sodium are types of this class.

Potassium, in particular, has such an affinity for oxygen, that on a piece being thrown into water, it immediately robs it of its oxygen, which unites with the metal, forming the oxide of potassium, or potash, and with such avidity, that the intense heat developed by the union of the two elements causes the hydrogen—the other constituent of water, and which is an inflammable gas—to ignite, and in this way actually the water may be said to burn. To set the Thames on fire, therefore, might easily be an accomplished fact. Regarding our further inquiries as to the elementary character of matter, of course it would be useless to attempt here to offer even a partial description of the various characteristics of all these elementary substances. It would need volumes to tell of all their unions and combinations; it would comprehend, in fact, within its limits the whole study of chemistry. However, to pàss by this part of our subject without notice, would be to err equally in the opposite direction. We purpose, then, to select from the list two of the most important elementary substances, one of which shall represent the metals, and the other the metalloids, and the two we propose are iron and oxygen; of the latter we shall first speak.

Oxygen, perhaps, of all the elementary substances, is the most widely diffused and important body throughout nature. It is this gas that supports life and combustion, and without its presence, all things living, whether animal or vegetable, must cease to exist. That such is the case is easily demonstrated. If, for instance, a bird, a mouse, or any other small animal, be confined in a perfectly air-tight receiver, it will continue to live until it has exhausted all the oxygen from the air; but when this takes place, it will die, and it will be found that a lighted taper placed in the receiver will be immediately extinguished; thus clearly proving that, in the absence of oxygen, life could not exist, or combustion take place. Oxygen unites with other simple bodies, giving an acid, basic, or neutral result.

Iron, for instance, combining with oxygen, forms a basic combination known as the oxide of iron, or, more commonly, rust (FeO).

Carbon unites with oxygen, forming an acid and a neutral body; as an acid, as carbonic acid (CO_2), and neutral as carbonic oxide, or oxide of carbon (CO), the latter having one equivalent less of oxygen. When charcoal, during combustion, has a sufficient supply of air, then carbonic acid, or CO_2, is formed; but if there is a deficiency of air, then three grains of carbon unite with only half as much oxygen, namely, with four grains instead of eight, and there is produced but half-made carbonic acid, as it were, which is called carbonic oxide$=(CO)$.

Carbonic oxide gas is extremely poisonous when inhaled. It burns, when kindled, with a blue flame, and so takes up the deficiency of oxygen, not supplied to it by the air while forming, and is converted into carbonic acid; that is, it takes up as much oxygen again, and CO becomes CO_2.

Carbonic acid, until very recently, was only known to chemists in its gaseous condition; but by great compression at a low temperature it has been condensed into a liquid, but which evaporates so quickly when the pressure is removed, that a cold of about 212° F (100° C) is produced. Owing to this, chemists have been enabled to render it solid. In fact, it becomes frozen, and has all the appearance of snow or ice.

Perhaps one of the greatest manifestations of natural economy, which is everywhere displayed throughout creation, is the balance which is constantly kept up between the animal and the vegetable world. For, whereas all animals inhale oxygen and exhale carbonic acid, vegetation inhales the carbonic acid and exhales the oxygen—the one giving off what the other needs, and retaining that which in too large quantities would prove injurious to the other. Were it not so, the constant consumption of the oxygen from the air by mankind and the whole of the animal kingdom in general, and the replacing it by carbonic acid, would, in the course of time, deteriorate the air to such an extent that life would gradually die out from the face of the earth, and would eventually become extinct. To prevent the possibility of such a catastrophe occurring, this all-wise provision has been made.

Another very important combination with oxygen is sulphur. It produces two acids— sulphuric (SO_3) and sulphurous (SO_2). Sulphuric acid is produced by the union of sulphur with oxygen, in the proportion of one of sulphur to three of oxygen; and sulphurous acid, one of sulphur to two of oxygen. Sulphurous acid, therefore, has one atom less oxygen than sulphuric.

"What iron is to the machinist, sulphuric acid is to the chemist. As the former makes out of iron not only machinery of all sorts, but also tools by which he can work up every other material, so sulphuric acid has also for us a double interest. It not only forms with the bases very important salts, but we employ it also as the most useful chemical means for producing numerous other chemical substances and changes. It stands, as it were, the Hercules among the acids, and by it we are able to overpower all others, and expel them from their combinations. It occurs in commerce as a liquid only. There are two sorts—(1) an oily, fuming liquid, Nordhausen sulphuric acid; and (2) another somewhat thinner, and not fuming acid, common sulphuric acid, or oil of vitriol."*

It is also obtainable in a solid state (anhydrous sulphuric acid) by removing the absorbed water which it contains by distillation. Sulphuric acid eagerly absorbs water from the air to the extent of two to three times its own

* Stockhardt's "Experimental Chemistry."

bulk. This may readily be proved by exposing some in an open vessel to the air. It will be found, after a week or two has elapsed, to have greatly increased; and supposing the vessel to have been half filled, it would, at the expiration of that time, in all probability, be found overflowing the sides.

Oxygen unites with various other bodies, forming acids of more or less importance to the chemist: with nitrogen, for instance, producing two acids, nitric acid or the aquafortis of the ancients (NO_5), being composed of one atom of nitrogen to five atoms of oxygen; and nitrous acid (NO_3), containing two atoms less oxygen than nitric. However, we must now pass on to notice how largely oxygen enters into the composition of the common things around us.

We have already noticed the important position it occupies in the atmosphere, being one fifth of its entire volume. It is a singular fact that the very gases which form this life-sustaining element which we breathe, and call air, should combine in other proportions and produce one of the most corrosive fluids known to chemists. Almost every one has heard of the astonishing effects produced by inhaling nitrous oxide (NO), or what is more commonly known as laughing gas; but it may be surpris-

ing to know that it only differs from the air by
containing one volume more oxygen in its
composition. By this we learn what an important difference a slight alteration in the
physical constitution of a body may make.
Water is a combination of oxygen and hydrogen,
and covers two-thirds of the earth's surface.
Oxygen enters largely into the composition of
very nearly all things—animal, vegetable, and
mineral.

The sand and pebbles of the sea-shore, the
flints from the chalk, and the immense beds
of sandstone, all consist chiefly of oxygen in
combination with the non-metallic element
silicon (Si), in the proportion of one atom of
silicon to three of oxygen. Flint, therefore,
in chemistry is known as silicic acid (SiO_3).
And although to some it may seem astonishing
that such substances as sand and flints should
be classed with the acids, yet the reason is
obvious, because, in common with all other
acids, it unites with bases forming salts. It
is often found beautifully crystallized in six-
sided prisms, and is known as rock crystal.
Many precious stones consist of this silicic
acid, their colours being due to the presence
of various metallic oxides.

Oxygen enters largely also into the composition of chalk. Chalk consists of lime

chemically combined with carbonic acid; and lime is a combination of oxygen with the metal calcium, and in chemical language is known as the oxide of calcium. " We find just the same constituents also in common limestone, in marble, oyster shells, &c. There are whole ridges of mountains consisting of limestone, and extensive districts having a lime or calcareous soil; carbonate of lime is one of the principal constituents of our globe. We also find it in transparent crystalline forms, rhombohedrous and six-sided prisms, and then call it calcareous spar. . . . .

" All limestones effervesce when treated with an acid, and may thus generally be distinguished from other stones. If you smear a piece of limestone in single spots with fat or some varnish paint, and then pour upon it an acid (a weak solution of nitric acid is the best), the lime dissolves in those places only which are unprotected by the fat or paint, the greasy spots accordingly remain raised. If a stone thus prepared is passed over with printing-ink, this will adhere only to the elevated places, and may be transferred from them to paper. This is the method used for engraving on stone, and the limestones used in this kind of engraving are called lithographic stones."[*]

[*] Stockhardt's " Experimental Chemistry."

..There are many other combinations with oxygen, which have more or less important applications, but we must beware of digressing. And although oxygen plays an equally important part in the organic world, we dare not venture into organic chemistry further than to state, that from the four elements— *carbon, hydrogen, oxygen,* and *nitrogen* (which are called the *organogens*)—are produced the countless multitudes of trees and plants which cover the surface of the globe, and are the principal elements in the physical constitution of all animal life as well. Oxygen in both cases playing an equally important part.

We have thus shown how largely oxygen, the most important of the metalloids, enters into the composition of the globe; but in treating oxygen as a type or representative of the metalloids, we must not be supposed to infer that they are necessarily all gaseous too. On the contrary, the majority of them are solid substances; indeed, some of them are so like metals that those who are not acquainted with the fact of their dissimulation, mistake them for metals. However, "there is a general agreement among chemists to divide simple bodies into *metalloids* and *metals*, but it is somewhat difficult to state with precision the characters on which this division is founded."

Metals are opaque, and possess a peculiar brightness, termed *metallic lustre*. They are good conductors of heat and electricity, which properties the metalloids do not possess in the same degree. This method of division is founded on properties which are not absolute, and which are more or less developed in the different elementary bodies. There are bodies which might, as regards their qualities, be classed with either one or the other; as arsenic, for example, which, in its chemical properties, approaches so closely to phosphorus, that many chemists include it among the metalloids, although it possesses the distinguishing characteristic of metals, metallic lustre, to quite as great an extent as many of the recognised metals. Carbon, again, assumes different appearances; in some cases it presents none of the appearances of metals, and is a very bad conductor of heat and electricity. In other cases, on the contrary, as in the instance of graphite, it possesses metallic lustre to a considerable extent, and is a very good conductor of electricity. Good conductors of heat and electricity are found only among those metals which possess the qualities of fusibility, ductility, and malleability in high perfection; those metals which have only been obtained in a pulverulent state being very indifferent conductors.

" In the binary combinations which metals form with metalloids, *the latter always act as the electro-negative element.* Both metals and metalloids combine with oxygen; the combinations of the former with oxygen are almost always *electro-positive oxides*, which act as *bases;* these generally contain the smallest proportion of oxygen. Some of them, which contain a larger proportion, act as *indifferent oxides;* and those which contain the largest proportion are not unfrequently acids, which form true salts with basic oxides.

" The metalloids, in combining with oxygen, generally form *indifferent oxides*, or *acid combinations.* Still, some of these combinations behave as bases—very feeble, certainly, in relation to strong acids. These same combinations act as weak acids with energetic bases. It will be seen, therefore, how narrow the line is which separates the metals from the metalloids." *
Taking, then, iron as the type of the metals, in the same way as we have been considering oxygen as a metalloid, we shall first briefly notice in what state, or rather in what combinations, it is naturally found; and then consider the many useful applications to which it is particularly adapted.

The principal combinations of iron are with

* Photographic News, Vol. III., p. 54.

oxygen. But the iron ores are never entirely pure, but always contain foreign ingredients (gangues)—such as silica, clay, lime, manganese, and others. Silica, more than any other, forms a principal ingredient, and is present in large quantities in most iron ores. And it is the presence of silica which makes the reducing of the iron so much more difficult, as it does not melt even when exposed to the most intense furnace heat. The consequence is, that it necessitates the addition of a base (commonly lime), with which the silicic acid will enter into combination, and in that state passes off as a kind of glass (lime glass).

The following are the combinations of iron with oxygen which are found in the various ores :—

Protoxide and sesquioxide of iron ($FeO + Fe_2O_3$), as in the magnetic iron ore. Carbonate of protoxide of iron ($FeO.CO_2$), as in clay ironstone, or spathic iron ore, from which the celebrated Styrian steel is principally prepared. Sesquioxide of iron, in combination with water ($Fe_2O_3 + 3HO$), as in the brown iron ore, yellow ochre, and yellow ironstone.

And, finally, the sesquioxide of iron alone (Fe_2O_3), as in red hematite iron glance, &c. (specular iron).

Almost all black and green stones, such as

clay-slate, greenstone, serpentine, &c., owe their colour to the presence of the protoxide of iron. Iron, indeed, is everywhere present on the earth, to a greater or lesser extent : in all stones and soils ; in almost every plant ; and is an ever-present constituent of the body, especially the blood, and from which it derives its colour.

The importance of iron for organic life has, we think, been much overlooked; and we think that much sickness and disease might be attributed to its deficiency in the human body. Certain it is, we find that the lives of workers in iron are very far above the average of any employed in any other branch of trade.

Considering the many uses to which iron is applied, of course it would be impossible here to enumerate all its applications ; we may, however, just glance at some of the most important.

Iron is used now to such an extent that the present (deservedly so, we think) has been called the " iron age."

The application of iron to the implements of agriculture is, perhaps, the most important; inasmuch as, without its agency, farming would almost become a dead lock.

Its uses in machinery, and its application to the arts and sciences, cannot be overrated. Without it, steam navigation would cease, and

locomotion become a blank.   Without it, too,
warfare would become but a puny thing in
comparison to what it is; truly, its horrors
would be assuaged, but the advantage here
could in no way compensate for its loss.   Even
for domestic purposes its loss would be severely
felt; and, finally, without it, the world would
be reduced to a state of semi-barbarity.

The following is a systematic synopsis of the
compounds of iron :—

Carburetted Iron.
(*a.*) Wrought iron (iron + ½ per cent. of carbon).
(*b.*) Cast iron   (iron + 5   „   „   ).
(*c.*) Steel, a mixture of both.

Sulphurets of Iron.
(*a.*) Protosulphuret of iron, black.
(*b.*) Bisulphuret of iron, yellow.
(*c.*) Sesquisulphuret of iron, mixture of both.

Oxides of Iron.
(*a.*) Protoxide of iron, black.
— Hydrated protoxide of iron, white.
(*b.*) Sesquioxide of iron, reddish brown.
— Hydrated sesquioxide of iron, yellowish brown.
(*c.*) Magnetic oxide of iron, black.
(*d.*) Ferric acid.

SALTS OF IRON (oxygen salts).
Salts of the Protoxide.
Sulphate of the protoxide of iron.
Nitrate   „   „
Carbonate   „   „
Acetate   „   „
Phosphate   „   „

Salts of the Sesquioxide.
Sulphate of the sesquioxide of iron.
Nitrate   „   „
Acetate   „   „
Phosphate   „   „

Haloid Salts.

Protochloride of iron.
Sesquichloride of iron.
Ferrocyanide of iron, blue
Ferrocyanide of potassium, yellow.
Ferrocyanide of copper, red.
Ferrocyanide of potassium, red.

We have thus given a description of the two most important elements. The following is a list of the elementary substances, with the chemical symbols by which they are known:—

TABLE OF EQUIVALENTS AND ATOMIC WEIGHTS OF THE SIMPLE OR ELEMENTARY BODIES.

In the following table, the numbers contained in columns I. and II. are deduced from those given by Berzelius, in the fifth edition of his *Lehrbuch;* and in column III. those Atomic Weights are added which Gerhardt and Laurent have quoted in the first number of the fifth volume of their *Comptes Rendus.*

Name of the Element.	Symbols.	I.—Equivalents.		II.—Atomic Weights.		III.—Equivalents (after Gerhardt and Laurent).	
		O. = 100.	H. = 1.	O.=100.	H. = 1.	O. = 100.	H.= 1.
Aluminium	Al.	170·900	13·694	170·900	27·388	85·63	13·70
Antimony	Sb.	1512·903	129·239	806·452	129·239	403·25	64·50
Arsenicum	As.	938·800	75·224	469·400	75·224	468·50	75·00
Barium	Ba.	855·290	68·533	855·290	137·066	425·00	68·00
Bismuth	Bi.	1330·377	106·600	1330·377	213·200	1312·50	210·00
Boron	B.	136·204	10·914	136·204	21·828	67·50	10·80
Bromine	Br.	999·620	80·098	499·810	80·098	500·00	80·00
Cadmium........	Cd.	696·767	55·831	696·767	111·662	350·00	56·00
Calcium	Ca.	251·651	20·164	250·000	40·000	125·00	20·00
Carbon...........	C.	75·120	6·019	75·120	12·038	75·00	12·00
Cerium (*Marignac*)	Ce.	590·800	47·264	590·800	94·528	—	—
Chlorine	Cl.	443·280	35·517	221·640	35·517	221·87	35·50
Chromium	Cr.	328·870	26·352	328·870	52·704	62·50	26·00
Cobalt	Co.	368·650	29·539	368·650	59·078	185·00	29·60
Copper...........	Cu.	395·600	31·699	395·600	63·398	198·75	31·80
Didymium (*Marignac*)	D.	620·000	49·600	620·000	99·200	—	—
Erbium	E.	—	—	—	—	—	—
Fluorine	Fl.	235·435	18·865	117·717	18·865	116·85	18·60

TABLE OF EQUIVALENTS, &c.—*continued.*

Name of the Element.	Symbols.	I.—Equivalents.		II.—Atomic Weights.		III.—Equivalents (after Gerhardt and Laurent).	
		O. = 100.	H. = 1.	O. = 100.	H. = 1.	O. = 100.	H. = 1.
Gold.............	Au.	2458·330	196·982	1229·165	196·982	1225·00	196·00
Glucinium	G.	87·124	6·981	87·124	10·962	—	—
Hydrogen	H.	12·480	1·300	6·240	1·000	6·25	1·00
Iodine	I.	1585·992	127·082	792·996	127·082	787·50	126·00
Iridium	Ir.	1232·080	98·724	1232·080	197·448	—	—
Iron...............	Fe.	350·527	28·087	350·527	56·174	175·00	28·00
Lanthanium (*Marignac*)...	La.	588·000	47·040	588·000	94·080	—	—
Lead	Pb.	1294·645	103·738	1294·645	207·476	650·00	104·00
Lithium	Li.	81·660	6·543	81·660	13·086	40·16	6·40
Magnesium	Mg.	158·140	12·671	158·140	25·342	75·00	12·00
Manganese	Mn.	344·684	27·619	344·684	55·288	175·00	28·00
Mercury	Hg.	1251·290	100·026	1250·000	200·000	625·00	100·00
Molybdenum ...	Mo.	596·100	47·764	596·100	95·528	—	—
Nickel	Ni.	369·330	29·594	369·330	59·188	185·00	29·60
Niobium	Nb.	—	—	—	—	—	—
Nitrogen	N.	175·060	14·027	87·530	14·027	87·50	14·00
Norium	No.	—	—	—	—	—	—
Osmium	Os.	1242·624	99·569	1242·624	199·138	—	—
Oxygen	O.	100·000	8·000	100·000	16·000	100·00	16·00
Palladium	Pd.	665·477	53·323	665·477	106·646	—	—
Pelopium	Pe.	—	—	—	—	—	—
Phosphorus......	P.	392·041	31·414	196·021	31·414	200·00	32·00
Platinum..........	Pt.	1232·080	98·724	1232·080	197·448	618·75	99·00
Potassium	K.	488·856	39·171	488·856	78·342	243·75	39·00
Rhodium	R.	651·962	52·240	651·962	104·326	—	—
Ruthenium (acc. to *Claus*)	Ru.	651·000	52·163	651·000	104·326	—	—
Selenium	Se.	495·285	39·686	495·285	79·372	490·90	78·50
Silicium	Si.	277·778	22·258	277·778	44·516	87·50	14·00
Silver	Ag.	1349·660	108·146	1349·660	216·292	675·00	108·00
Sodium	Na.	289·729	23·215	289·729	46·430	143·75	23·00
Sulphur	S.	200·750	16·086	200·750	32·171	200·00	32·00
Strontium	Sr.	545·929	43·744	545·929	87·488	275·00	44·00
Tantalium, *or* Columbium }	Ta.	1148·365	92·016	1148·365	184·032	—	—
Tellurium	Te.	801·760	64·244	801·760	128·488	800·00	128·00
Terbium	Tb.	—	—	—	—	—	—
Thorium	Th.	743·860	59·604	743·860	119·208	—	—
Titanium..........	Ti.	301·550	24·158	301·550	48·316	—	—
Tin	Sn.	735·294	58·918	735·294	117·836	368·75	59·00
Tungsten..........	W.	1188·360	95·22	188·360	190·442	600·00	96·00
Uranium	U.	742·885	59·525	742·875	119·050	750·00	120·00
Vanadium	V.	856·892	68·661	856·892	137·322	—	—
Yttrium	Y.	—	—	—	—	—	—
Zinc..............	Zn.	406·591	32·579	406·591	65·158	206·25	33·00
Zirconium	Zr.	419·728	33·632	419·728	67·264	—	—

The substances in the above list which have not the equivalent and atomic weights annexed to them, are those bodies which have, as yet, not been reduced to their simple elementary conditions, and consequently their equivalents and atomic weights have not been ascertained. It is, then, from these elementary substances that the entire universe is constituted. And no matter under what forms or distinctions things may be characterised, whether organic or inorganic, they will, one and all, be found compounded from these elementary bodies, which collectively form the basis of the "*physical constitution of the universe.*"

ESSAY V.

ON MATTER AND ITS PROPERTIES.

THE ATOMIC THEORY; ITS GREEK ORIGIN—INFINITE DIVISIBILITY OF MATTER—ATTRACTION OF GRAVITATION—RECIPROCAL ATTRACTION — CAPILLARY ATTRACTION — ATTRACTION OF COHESION — CHEMICAL ATTRACTION — COMPOSITION OF THE DIAMOND—MAGNETIC AND ELECTRIC ATTRACTION—HEAT; LATENT AND APPRECIABLE—WEIGHT OF BODIES—DENSITY—SPECIFIC GRAVITY—PROPERTIES OF METALS AND OTHER SUBSTANCES—MOTION AND FORCES.

MATTER assumes three distinct forms—solid, liquid, and gaseous. Solid, as the earth; liquid, as water; and gaseous, as the air; and each of these distinguishing features possesses properties widely differing from the other; but whatever properties matter may possess, or wherever it is manifested to us, it must necessarily assume one of these three distinguishing characteristics. However, there are properties which are common to matter in whatever form it may assume.

And, to commence with, all matter is composed of atoms, or infinitely small particles, which are not capable of being subdivided. The word "atom" is derived from the Greek, and means that which cannot be cut into smaller particles, and it is to the ancient Greek philosophers, more especially, that we owe the origin of the atomic theory; and however abstruse and inventive their theories generally were, and unaccompanied by that which so pre-eminently distinguishes our own times, experimental research, still they were very searching inquirers into the secrets of nature, and by a bold kind of speculative philosophy they often arrived at a portion of the truth, which, in later times, has been extenuated and proven. However, all philosophical investigations should be as much as possible divested of all vagueness of idea, and limited to actual observation and experiment.

"All that can rightly be called atomic philosophy — the investigation of matter in its molecular parts, and under the different combinations and mutual actions of these—comes distinctly within the field of legitimate inquiry. Yet here, too, rash speculation had a long period of supremacy. We have already alluded to those hypotheses of the Greek philosophers, through which, unaided by experiment, they

sought to explain the multiform shapes, combinations, and changes which matter assumes
or undergoes. They saw, as it was easy to see,
that for such an explanation it must be supposed divisible into parts of exquisite minuteness, since under no other conception than
this, are phenomena of possible fulfilment. It
was further seen, and almost by the same
necessity, that these minute parts, molecules,
or atoms, must have definite relations, whether
of attraction or repulsion, to one another. All
nature, animate or inanimate, teems with evidence to this effect, and no experiment was
needed to attest it. The conception of definite
proportions in their molecular relations—now
ripened into a great physical law—can hardly
be said to occur in the ancient philosophy,
though some few passages may vaguely express
the idea. But another question, yet current
in our own time, and which lies at the bottom
of every atomic theory, engaged more distinctly
the notice of these schools of antiquity—a
question which neither reason nor experiment
can ever do more than settle presumptively,
viz., whether there are truly ultimate molecules, or atoms of matter, unsusceptible of
further division, or whether we must here, as
elsewhere in nature, veil our reason before that
metaphysical infinite which baffles alike defini-

tion and conception, and consider matter as divisible without limit or end?"*

The advocates of each of these theories have recently provoked much scientific discussion, and, according to our minds, without the least effect, both leaving off where they commenced, and each adhering to their own individual ideas on the subject. The infinite divisibility of matter is so purely a metaphysical inquiry, that we give it up at once for the more probable, and certainly the more reasonable theory, of atomic particles of matter, which, however inconceivably minute, are nevertheless absolute units in themselves, and are incapable of any further division.

The experiments of Dalton and others, respecting the atomic weights of simple bodies and their combinations, are of the greatest interest and importance. The fact arrived at is this: that when simple bodies enter into combination one with another, they always do so in fixed proportions, which proportions must either be equal to, or multiples of, one another, and in no other proportions can they combine.

The immense divisibility of matter will give some idea of the almost infinite minuteness to which matter may be reduced. One single

* Holland's Essays (article, "Life of Dalton"), p. 409.

grain of gold, mixed with one pound of molten silver, will become disseminated through the entire mass. It, therefore, follows that one grain of this silver will contain the one 5,760th part of a grain of gold, that being the number of grains to a pound.

It would require nearly three hundred thousand leaves of gold to become one inch thick; in other words, the ordinary gold leaf used in gilding is proved to be little more than the three hundred thousandth part of an inch in thickness. Again, one single grain of gold is made to cover ten thousand square inches, in covering the silver wire used in making gold lace, and is then only the four millionth part of an inch in thickness.

In experimenting on platinum, Dr. Wollaston succeeded in drawing such fine wires, that one hundred and forty of them were only the thickness of a single fibre of silk.

Newton has proved that the delicate film of a soap-bubble, consisting of water with a hundredth part of its bulk of soap, is not more than the two million six hundred thousandth part of an inch in thickness.

As far as man can penetrate into the minuteness of nature, with the utmost help of his ingenuity, he discovers living animals, perfect in formation, active in their movements, obeying natural laws, and yet a million of them do not take up more space than a grain of sand. Each of these must be again divisible; and who can say they are the smallest of animal formation? Part of the towns of Berlin in Europe, and of Richmond and Petersburg in America, stand on a bed of earth which the microscope has proved to be a mass of fossil animalcula: how wonderfully minute, when a handful contains billions of individuals once possessed of organs of digestion, motion, feeling, and reproduction!

The fine polishing powder called tripoli, so largely used in the arts, consists entirely of the invisible siliceous shells of animals: how inconceivably small must each part of them be, when 220 grains contain " upwards of forty thousand millions of individual organisms!" The mud thrown up yearly on the banks of the "hoary Nile" does not result, as was supposed, from the washed-down *débris* of the mountains; but is composed almost entirely of a multitudinous accumulation of infinitely minute living forms of animal life, wholly undiscernible to the naked eye in themselves, but in a mass constituting no inconsiderable portion of the solid soil. Who, then, can set a limit even to the divisibility of organic matter? A man could hold in his hand more of these animalcules than there are of mankind in the whole world. Minute, however, as we have shown many things to be, there are some, sensible to our senses, still more so. Odour is known to be the disengagement of particles of a substance ; small, then, must be the atoms of musk ! During twenty years, a grain has perfumed an apartment where the air was frequently changed; and after all these years, diffusing itself into millions of cubic feet of air, its diminution of weight could hardly be estimated.*

If such, then, is the extent of the appreciable divisibility of matter, what must be the size of those still infinitely smaller particles which we choose to call atoms ? Having thus given a kind of outline of the atomic theory and pronounced our opinion thereon, we shall now direct the attention of our readers more particularly to the various properties which matter possesses.

We shall start with the great universal law of attraction, or gravitation, propounded by Newton from the falling of an apple, which induced this philosophical reasoner to investigate the law which governed its fall, and from which simple incident, it is said, we are indebted for the discovery of this important law.

Now, as each atom is supposed to be isolated from the rest, no two particles of matter touch.

* Elements of Experimental and Natural Philosophy.

Sir John Herschel thought it probable that the atoms composing a body were not more thickly scattered through its mass than are the stars through space; and Newton gave it as his opinion, that could the earth be so compressed as to bring each atom in conjunction, its dimensions might not exceed a cubic inch.

If this be the case, then, how wonderful is the power which holds these atoms together, and makes them assume the beautiful and varied forms with which we are surrounded. This is perhaps the finest, the noblest instance of the universality of the laws of nature; the same attractive power which holds the stars in their places, binds the atoms into masses and preserves their forms.

However, notwithstanding the universality of the law of attraction, we find it varies considerably in force; if, for instance, we take a piece of chalk, and a piece of marble—bodies whose chemical combinations are precisely similar—we shall find that the particles of the one are much more firmly held together than the other. The chalk will readily crumble to pieces with but a slight pressure of the fingers, whilst the marble will require a far greater power than the fingers possess to reduce it to a pulverized condition.

The law of attraction is reciprocal; that is,

one body attracts another, in exactly the same proportion as it is by it attracted, and the attractive force is inversely as the square of the distance; for instance, supposing anything to be removed twice the distance from the centre to the surface of the earth, the attractive power would be four times less, and it consequently would only weigh one fourth as much. In consequence of the earth being flattened at the poles, the attraction is $\frac{1}{590}$ greater than at the equator; but as there is no centrifugal force at the poles, the weight of bodies on that account will be increased $\frac{1}{385}$; therefore, the difference in weight between the equator and the poles will be $\frac{1}{195}$. Thus, a body weighing 195 lbs. at the equator, would weigh 196 lbs. on its being taken to the poles.

At present we have only been noticing the attraction of gravitation. There are, however, different kinds of attraction, as follows, viz.:—

Capillary attraction, cohesive and chemical, magnetic and electric attraction.

We shall briefly notice each of these in the order in which they stand.

First, then, capillary attraction signifies that kind of attraction which we observe in dipping a sponge or other porous substances in water, and which causes the water to rise and become disseminated through the entire mass. The word capillary is a derivation from the Latin word *capilla*—a hair; now a hair, as we all know, is a tube, and therefore the word capillary signifies the attraction of a fluid through tubes or pores. It is capillary attraction which causes the water to rise between two pieces of glass when placed with their faces nearly touching in a dish of water; the same thing takes place when glass tubes are similarly immersed. Bargemen, in dry weather, throw water on their sails, for the purpose of swelling the fibres, or capillary tubes, thus forming a closer texture to hold the wind. If a heavy weight be attached to a tight rope, in such a manner that it shall just rest on the ground, it may be raised considerably by simply wetting the rope.

Mr. Jabez Hogg, in his "Elements of Experimental and Natural Philosophy," gives the following excellent story, illustrative of the effects of moisture on ropes. Even if it be a romance tacked on to an historical fact, still it is so impressive of the truth of a principle that it merits notice.

"In the piazza before St. Peter's, at Rome, stands the most beautiful obelisk in the world. It was brought from the circus of Nero, where it had lain buried for many ages. It is one entire piece of Egyptian marble, 72 feet high,

12 feet square at the base, and 8 feet at the top, and is computed to weigh above 470 tons, and supposed to be upwards of 3,000 years old. Much engineering skill was required to remove and erect this piece of art, and the celebrated architect, Dominico Fontain, was selected and engaged by Pope Sextus V. to carry out this difficult operation.

" A pedestal, thirty feet high, was built for its reception, and the obelisk brought to its base. Many were the ingenious contrivances prepared for the raising it to its resting-place, all of which excited the deepest interest amongst the people. At length, everything was in readiness, and a day appointed for the great event. A great multitude assembled to witness the ceremony; and, afraid that the clamour and curiosity of the people might distract the attention of the architect, the Pope issued an edict, containing regulations to be observed, and imposing the severest penalties on any one who should, during the lifting of the gigantic stone, utter a single word. Amidst suppressed excitement of feelings and breathless silence, the splendid monument was gradually raised to within a few inches of the top of the pedestal, when its upward motion ceased; it hung suspended, and could not be got further ; the tackle was too short, and there seemed no other way than to undo the great work already accomplished. The annoyed architect, in his perplexity, hardly knew how to act, while the silent people were anxiously watching every motion of his features, to discover how the problem would be solved.

" In the crowd was an old British tar; he saw the difficulty, and how to overcome it: with stentorian lungs he shouted out—' Wet the ropes!' The vigilant police pounced on the culprit, and lodged him in prison. The architect caught the magic words; he put this proposition in force, and the cheers of the people proclaimed the success of the great undertaking. Next day, the English criminal was solemnly arraigned before his holiness; his crime was undeniably proved, and the Pope, in solemn language, pronounced the sentence to be—that he receive a pension annually during his lifetime."

Attraction of cohesion signifies the power which holds all bodies together; and without this power, matter "would form a universe of dust." It varies considerably in intensity in some substances, as we have previously observed with regard to chalk and marble. It exists in its greatest intensity in the metals; it is considerably less in stones, earths, and other solids of a like nature; and is weakest in fluids.

Chemical attraction, otherwise termed chemi-
-cal affinity, is that power which effects the
combination of simple bodies into compound
substances.   Here, also, we find it subject to
different variations, and producing altogether
dissimilar bodies, from the same combination.
Carbon shows us clearly how one and the same
body may have entirely different forms and
different proportions.   In common wood-char-
coal, animal-charcoal, and coke, it is *amorphous*
—that is, without any particular shape, and is
also very combustible.   In graphite, or plum-
bago—which we may call crystallized black
carbon—it possesses a peculiar structure, is
metallic in appearance, and is very nearly in-
combustible.   In the diamond—which is no
more nor less than crystallized colourless carbon—it is possessed of an entirely different
character: it is transparent, and crystallized
in four-sided double pyramids; it is very difficult of combustion under ordinary circumstances, but may be entirely burnt up in oxygen
gas; and the only product obtained from it is
carbonic acid gas, and in exactly the same
quantity as if an equally heavy piece of wood-
charcoal were similarly consumed.

The strongest heat is incapable of melting
charcoal, nor is there any liquid known by
which it may be dissolved.   Could it by any

means be rendered liquid, or any liquid found in which it would dissolve, then, assuredly, could diamonds be artificially produced. The diamond, however, and carbon are both simple bodies, the atoms only being differently arranged, yet the difference in their forms is greater than is observable in bodies which are entirely distinct. And atoms of different substances will not unite in the same way as atoms of the same kind do, there being apparently greater affinity between some than others; and when atoms of different kinds combine, the combination resulting from their union generally loses all resemblance to the substances combining. For instance, sulphuric acid unites with iron, forming a salt of a beautiful emerald green colour; with copper the salt is blue. The affinity, however, is greater with the iron, which is proved by throwing a piece of iron into a solution of the copper salt; in the course of time the copper will be entirely deposited at the bottom of the vessel in a fine powder, whilst the solution will have changed from the sulphate of copper to the sulphate of iron, the iron having been taken up during the deposition of the copper. This illustrates partly the theory of electro-metallurgy. Magnetic and electrical attraction we regard as mere modifications of the same power; this is strikingly exemplified in the induction of magnetism by a voltaic current, and still further so by the induction of electricity by magnetism.

" The most remarkable property of a magnet is the power it possesses of attracting iron, to the exclusion of nearly all other substances. The metals nickel and cobalt are, indeed, also attracted by the magnet, but in so much lower a degree that the power, practically speaking, may be said to be limited to iron."* Whereas electrical attraction extends its influence in and upon all things.

Another very important and universal property of matter, is heat; it is the great modifying power of the universe, and extends its influence through all things, and according to its intensity or diminution, the form and condition of all material things depend. Take water, for instance, which at a certain reduced temperature is solid; an increase of heat renders it liquid, and a still greater elevation produces steam. All other substances behave in a similar manner; that is, as far as we know from actual experiment. There are, of course, many substances which defy the most intense heat at our disposal to become either liquid or gaseous. But there can be no doubt that at a

* Bakewell's " Electricity."

certain elevation of temperature—of the intensity of which we can have but a faint idea—all things would become aëriform or gaseous. All bodies expand on an elevation of temperature, and, with one single exception, all bodies contract on its withdrawal. This exception is in the solidification of water (freezing), and in so doing it expands, as is proved by the bursting of vessels containing it. It is, indeed, a wise provision, for otherwise the water in our rivers would, on becoming frozen on the surface, immediately sink to the bottom, and would thus in a short time render them entirely unnavigable, and some considerable time would have to elapse ere it would become thawed.

Heat assumes two important conditions.

First, latent or hidden heat; and second, manifested or appreciable heat. Latent heat is that kind of heat which lies dormant, and pervades all things; we are insensible of its presence until certain means be adopted for setting it free. It is latent heat which is developed upon rubbing a metal button on a smooth surface. Two pieces of ice on being rubbed together will melt from the latent heat being set free. A piece of iron may be beaten by a hammer until it is nearly red hot. In some countries the natives produce fire by merely rubbing two pieces of wood together.

This is entirely caused from the liberation of the heat which actually exists in the wood in a latent condition. We regard the existence of heat in the same light as electricity. Heat and electricity are everywhere present, and both are developed by friction, or otherwise exciting the particles of matter. Perhaps the most extraordinary example of the presence of latent heat, occurs in high-pressure steam; when steam is subjected to a great pressure, and then allowed to escape, the hand is not sensible of any heat when held in it near the outlet, but at a little distance away it would produce a scald, the heat redeveloping itself on the expansion of the vapour.

Manifested or appreciable heat and its effects are too well known to need description. We derive heat from the rays of the sun; our own bodies testify as to its presence; and, besides which, we know of it from the various artificial ways, we may say, of producing it. We shall, therefore, leave it, and pass on to notice other properties of matter, which are not so generally known.

Weight is a property possessed by all bodies, although in a variable degree. Actually, however, there is no such thing as weight—it is only a term we use to express the difference in the specific gravity of bodies. For it must be understood that, apart from the gravitating influence exercised by the earth on all things on its surface, there would be no such thing as weight. Matter in itself is not possessed of weight; and could anything be taken to the centre of the earth, it would be found not to weigh anything, simply because it would have reached the centre of the gravitating influence which produces the phenomena we call weight. The difference in the weight of bodies arises from the variation in their densities and specific gravity.

The density of a body signifies the difference existing in the closeness or compactness of its particles. The weight of a handful of feathers is comparatively trifling, when compared with its bulk; but many people would be surprised at the immense weight of a compressed bale of the same: by the pressure they are made more dense.

A mixture of tin and copper will occupy one-fifteenth less space than they took up when unmixed: the density of the mass is increased.

We have in our possession pieces of the wreck of the "Royal George," which, by the continued pressure of the water, have become so dense, that they will now sink in water like a piece of iron. An increase of density, then, produces a relative increase of weight.

What we mean by specific gravity, is the difference existing in the weights of bodies, taking volume for volume. For instance, a pound of water and a pound of lead are necessarily of the same weight, but a pint of water and a pint of lead widely differ—the lead being eleven times heavier than the water. This is termed the difference in their specific gravity.

Water, distilled, has been taken as the standard from which all others are judged, as in all places at a given temperature, and the barometer at a certain height, it is always exactly the same. The following shows the difference in the specific gravity of certain bodies, including the most important metals:—

1 volume water	=	1
1 „ sulphur	=	2
1 „ bromine	=	3
1 „ diamond	=	$3\frac{1}{2}$
1 „ iodine	=	5
1 „ tin	=	7
1 „ iron	=	$7\frac{1}{2}$
1 „ manganese	=	8
1 „ copper	=	$8\frac{1}{2}$
1 „ nickel	=	9
1 „ bismuth	=	10
1 „ silver	=	$10\frac{1}{2}$
1 „ lead	=	11
1 „ mercury	=	$13\frac{1}{2}$
1 „ gold	=	19
1 „ platinum	=	$21\frac{1}{2}$

It will be seen from this list that the metal platinum is the heaviest—or, in other words, it has the greatest specific gravity. Hitherto we have been describing properties which are general and universal to matter, in whatever forms or conditions it may exist. We have now to describe certain properties which distinguish some forms of matter from others.

The class of substances known as metals have many distinguishing properties, and many metals possess properties which are either altogether wanting in others, or else only possessed to a very limited degree. Metallic lustre is a property possessed by all.

Tenacity is a property possessed more particularly by the metals, although all substances possess it to a certain degree; it signifies the extent of the resistance which matter is capable of sustaining when forces are exerted upon it in opposite directions.

The tenacity of metals is tested by the amount of weight which wires of a given thickness will sustain. Thus, wires measuring one-tenth of an inch in diameter, and made of the following metals, will sustain the various weights appended to them before they will break, and by this means the different degrees of tenacity are estimated, viz. :—

Iron	549 lbs.	Gold	150 lbs.
Copper	302 „	Zinc	109 „
Platinum	274 „	Tin	34 „
Silver............	187 „	Lead	27 „

From this table we find that iron possesses the greatest amount of tenacity, and therefore is admirably adapted for sustaining great weights. It is just double the strength of platinum, nearly three times the strength of silver, and more than twenty times the strength of lead.

A steel wire, of not more than the hundredth part of an inch in diameter, has been found capable of sustaining a weight of 130 lbs., without breaking.

" The great tenacity of iron has led to many improvements for the comfort, convenience, and prosperity of man. Wire ropes, from their extraordinary power, and combining lightness, are gradually being adopted in our maritime industry; iron cables, from their strength, and not having a direct pull on the vessel, but curving in the water from their own weight, which is gradually and gently overcome before there is a positive strain on the vessel, are entirely superseding hempen ones. Those spider-like webs, connecting mountain to mountain, forming a pathway in air—the suspension bridges, with vessels passing underneath—owe their value to the tenacity of iron. Two iron ropes, thousands of tons in weight, rising over towers eighty feet in height, stretch over the thundering rapids and fearful chasm of Niagara's Falls. On these wires are fixed scantlings, and resting upon them are light planks, forming a safe pathway ten feet in width.

"The latest and boldest effort of man's genius, in which iron is made the subservient instrument, is the wonderful tunnel, placed across an arm of the sea, forming a roadway for carriages, far above the tallest mast that is borne on the ocean underneath. In this newly-added 'wonder of the world,' the long-practised arch-formation of such structures is abandoned, and a level defies the elements and strain of man. The stubbornness of strength and firm cohesion of herculean iron, stretches from pier to pier, scarcely vibrating or crouching to tons upon tons of moving weight whirled through its sombre interior;—we are referring to the Britannia Bridge, which is another brilliant gem added to the civic crown of our indefatigable countrymen. It spans the sea 1,513 feet, at a height of 102 feet above the utmost rise of the waves, and of itself weighs 10,570 tons."*

* Elements of Experimental and Natural Philosophy. London: Ingram, Cooke, & Co.

Ductility is a property possessed by some metals, and not others, and signifies their capacity of being drawn out into wires.

Platinum, gold, silver, copper, and iron, are the principal metals possessing this distinguishing quality. We have already alluded to the fact of Dr. Wollaston having drawn platinum wires to the one-three-millionth of an inch in diameter.

Malleability, or the property of being beaten out, is also peculiar to some metals. Gold possesses it to a large extent, as we have mentioned in the operations of the gold-beater. Silver, copper, and tin likewise possess this property, almost in the same degree.

Pliability, or the capacity of being bent backwards and forwards without injury, is common to those metals which are also ductile.

These, then, are the distinguishing properties of certain of that class of bodies called metals. We shall, however, in passing, just notice one or two properties which characterise certain other bodies entirely dissimilar in appearance.

And, first of all, hardness is a property which many bodies possess over others.

It might be supposed that the density of a body would have much to do with its hardness, *i.e.*, the greater the density the greater the amount of hardness. Not so. Mercury, for instance, which is a liquid, is more dense than iron. And then, again, the diamond, which is the hardest body in nature, is only one-third the density of mercury.

Glass is also very hard, but the diamond is so much harder that it readily cuts it on being drawn across its surface. Closely associated with hardness is brittleness; as substances which are extremely hard are generally very brittle. Indeed, it seems to be a property acquired on things becoming hardened. Take steel, for instance, which, when gradually cooled, is both soft and pliable; but when cooled more quickly, acquires both hardness and brittleness. The two seem to be almost inseparably connected.

Glass, as we have just said, is hard, and it is, perhaps, the most brittle substance we have. And, again, wrought or bar iron may readily be bent, but not so readily broken; whereas cast iron, which is extremely hard, is easily chipped at the slightest blow from a hammer.

Impenetrability is the resistance which one body exerts on another when impelled against it by force; and it further signifies that the space occupied by one body cannot, at the same time, be occupied by another. Therefore, when one body is said to penetrate another, it simply means the displacement of the particles of the one from the force exerted on it by the other, in order that it may make its passage through it. The piston of a syringe cannot be pushed down, if the finger is placed on the outlet when the syringe is full of water. A bullet, when fired perpendicularly on the surface of water, is flattened from the impenetrability of its particles. The same bullet, fired through a piece of glass, would cut a perfectly round hole in it. In this case the particles are displaced, and carried away by the bullet's force. And, lastly, elasticity is a property possessed by various substances, by which they recover their former shapes after having been bent, or their particles otherwise altered. We call india rubber elastic, as, after being stretched or bent, it re-assumes its original shape.

Steel can be made extremely elastic, as the elasticity of some sword-blades would testify. The spring of a watch is also an example of the elasticity of steel, which for years will keep bending and re-assuming its former position. The most perfectly elastic body is glass, which being bent under pressure for many years, will immediately recover its shape on the pressure being removed.

Hidden in as great a mystery as the God-head, lie the great laws which govern the motion and forces of matter. We only know of their existence by the results they produce, but for the cause we vainly endeavour to investigate. There is but one true way of regarding the primary cause, and that is the one which points higher than human understanding can ascend, and leads us to recognise that Supreme and Almighty Power which overrules all things, and brings us to acknowledge these causes as attributes of the Deity.

Seeing, then, that the why and the wherefore must remain hidden from our scrutiny, all that we can attain to is the study of the effects produced, and the classification of the various laws by which these effects are governed. The most striking characteristic of motion is its universality; absolute rest is impossible, and things apparently still are actuated by forces which permeate the mass, and produce effects which, although unobservable to the eye, yet exist, and can be detected by other means. Even the variation of temperature produces a disturbing influence on all things, and every particle or atom composing a body is set in motion by the slightest elevation or decrease in heat. But, more than this, nothing can be

K

actually at rest, from the fact of the universal revolution of the earth and all the heavenly bodies round some centre. Things may be relatively at rest one with the other, but all must partake of this common motion. The immense pyramids of Egypt occupied exactly the same position relatively a thousand years ago as they do now, although actually they have changed their position in space probably millions upon millions of miles; and in common with all terrestrial objects they continually partake of the motion of the earth, first round its own axis, and secondly, in its revolution round the sun.

Force is equally wide-spread and universal—in fact, a great deal more so, for motion is no more nor less than the manifestation of force. Force can, and, of course, does exist alone. There can be force without motion, but it is impossible that there can be motion without force. Force more nearly expresses the great acting principle, while motion is but a consequence.

With these few remarks on the motion and forces of matter we must conclude, seeing that to proceed further to any investigation of them would involve us in excessively speculative and metaphysical inquiries, and which, as we have already intimated at the

commencement of this essay, we have a great
desire to avoid, as, in this instance, no good
could result from such speculations; and we
can, therefore, only look upon them as manifestations of an omnipotent Creator.

ESSAY VI.

ON THE IMMENSITY OF THE UNIVERSE.

SOLAR SYSTEM—THE SUN—INCANDESCENT ATMOSPHERE
—MERCURY—VENUS—THE EARTH AND ITS MOON
—MARS; RESEMBLANCE TO THE EARTH—THE AS-
TEROIDS—DISCOVERY BY PIAZZI—JUPITER AND ITS
SATELLITES—SATURN; ITS RING AND SATELLITES—
URANUS—NEPTUNE; ITS DISCOVERY BY ADAMS AND
LEVERIER—COMETS, CONSTITUTION OF; THEIR MOTIONS
—METEORS AND SHOOTING STARS—THE FIXED STARS
—THE MILKY WAY AND NEBULÆ.

WE have often been struck at the lightness
with which people regard things that are going
on around them, and constantly presented to
their notice: it is indeed remarkable; but
there are many, we think, who would scarcely
know the existence of an atmosphere in which
we live and move, were it not for a good
stiff breeze now and then to refresh their
memories.   Much less, however, do they take

notice of the stars, oh! dear no, *they* have nothing to do with *them*, that is the work of astronomers. Well, so far they are right; but how many astronomers should we have, think you, if every one said the same? But let us for a moment try to imagine that there are no stars nor moon to light the benighted traveller's path, and that after the sun had gone down it would leave a pitchy blackness behind. Fancy, if you can, such a night as this; and now let us suppose that these myriad sparkling orbs— which deck our skies from night to night -- could suddenly burst upon our view, that the moon with silvery rays could light up nature and make it radiant with joy, Oh! wonder of wonders, sight of sights, see earth with her teeming millions gazing upwards with astonishment and admiration. Can you fancy such a scene as this? It is because we get used to these things that makes us depreciate their value; but to the lover of nature they are ever a source of gratification and enjoyment. He loves to trace the planet in its course, to watch the setting sun. To him, the music of the stars sends forth higher strains than any earthly melody;

> " Ever singing, as they shine,
> The hand that made them is divine."

Perhaps, of all the sciences, the study of

astronomy is the most awe-inspiring and truly grand, and the one which points pre-eminently to the existence of an Infinite and Omnipotent Being. The immensity of the heavenly bodies, as well as the vastness of the celestial spaces, are such as to overwhelm the mind of man, to humble his pride from its grandeur and magnificence, and bid him recognise the handiwork of an eternal Creator. With these few remarks we shall commence our observations by describing the solar system, and make our starting point the glorious sun, the life and centre of the whole. "It is, of all the heavenly bodies, the one most frequently in our thoughts." It is the brightest thing which the Lord of Glory has been pleased to show us in this life; * so bright, indeed, that the most intensely brilliant light which modern science has discovered, appears—when placed before it—as a dark inky blotch on its effulgent surface.

"It is the fountain of colour, which gives its azure to the sky, its verdure to the fields, its rainbow hues to the gay world of flowers, and the 'purple light of love' to the marble cheek of youth and beauty."†

It is the source of light and heat to all the

* Royal Astronomical Society's Monthly Notice for January, 1859.

† More Worlds than One.

planets, and by its magnetic power supports them in their places; and could this power be suspended, but for one short hour, our earth, with all the other planets, would " wander darkling in the eternal space." This stupendous orb is 880,000 miles in diameter, or more than large enough—supposing it to be hollowed out—to contain our earth with its revolving moon; it is, in fact, 500 times larger than all the planets put together.

There can be no doubt that the sun is an opaque dark body, surrounded by an intensely brilliant atmosphere, consisting of matter in a state of incandescence; the idea of its being a huge body of fire has been for a long time abandoned. The observation of the dark spots on its surface, first noticed by Galileo in 1610, has thrown considerable light on the subject, for these spots are no more nor less than the dark body of the sun visible through the inner atmospheres; and caused, it is supposed, by enormous disturbances in the outer and luminous solar atmosphere. By the observation of these spots, also, has been established the fact of the revolution of the sun on its axis, which it accomplishes in twenty-five days.

And now, leaving our great starting-point, we pass on to notice the planets. The first, or nearest to the sun, is Mercury, situated at a dis-

tance of thirty-six millions of miles; it performs
a revolution round the sun in eighty-eight days,
and on its axis in twenty-four hours, making
the day the same length as ours. The dia -
meter of Mercury is about 3,200 miles.

"Mercury has been viewed with interest
from the earliest times, and under various
names has been worshipped by the heathen
nations of antiquity. Yet it is related that
Copernicus, who lived to attain his seventieth
year, never once succeeded in seeing Mercury,
and on his death-bed much regretted the
fact."*

"With a tolerably clear horizon, however,
Mercury may be observed even in our latitudes
for a few days every year. We scan the
Almanac till we find a morning in which
Mercury rises nearly two hours before the sun,
or an evening in which its setting follows that
of the sun by a similar interval."†

Its great brightness is a considerable drawback to telescopic observations, but some
astronomers state that they have observed spots
and irregularities on its surface, which from
their appearance have led them to suppose to
be mountains of several miles in height. Other
observers differ on this point, however, in the

---

* Cosmos, vol. iii., p 347.
† Telescopic Teachings, p. 86.

belief that the atmosphere is so overloaded with clouds as to prevent the body of the planet being seen.

" Next to Mercury, the planet Venus revolves at the distance of sixty-eight millions of miles, with a day of twenty-four hours, and a year of 225 days. Her diameter is 7,700 miles, a little less than that of the earth.* Venus, like Mercury, exhibits phases like the moon, but the time of its greatest brilliancy is not when it appears full; as it travels in its orbit to the position corresponding to ' half moon,' its apparent brightness increases, and the planet attains its greatest brilliancy when at a distance of forty degrees from the sun."†

" There is a beautiful tradition respecting the phases of Venus, which appears, however, to partake rather of the nature of an allegory, or illustration, than of an historical anecdote ! It is said that when Copernicus announced his theory of the solar system, it was objected that were his theory true, Venus ought, at certain positions in its orbit, to exhibit the various forms of the moon. The invention of the telescope had not then been dreamt of; but it is said that Copernicus, in a fine spirit of prophecy, answered, that should men ever see

* More Worlds than One, p. 21.
† Nichol's " Cyclopædia," p. 767.

Venus better, they would discern these phases. No mention is made of this story by Galileo, who discovered the varying forms of Venus in the year 1611, with the aid of the telescope, or by Gassendi, the biographer of Copernicus. Copernicus, indeed, was not spared to answer any objections to his system, as he barely lived to lay his hand upon a copy of his own work, and never opened it."*

We now come to notice our Earth, which is the third planet, and is distant from the sun 95,000,000 miles; its diameter from the equator, 7,926 miles; and from the poles nearly 7,900 miles,—a difference in the two diameters of a little more than thirty-six miles. It performs a revolution round the sun in somewhat over 365 days, and on its axis in twenty-four hours.

The Earth is the first planet accompanied by a satellite or moon, the distance of which is 237,000 miles, and 2,160 miles in diameter, and revolves round the Earth in twenty-eight days. The appearance the moon presents to us is remarkably uneven and mountainous. There are also enormous circular cavities, which have been computed to be as much as five miles in depth, and forty in diameter. Leaving our Earth, at a distance of 47,000,000

* Penny Cyclopædia.

miles, and 142,000,000 from the sun, we find the planet Mars—a comparatively small planet —being only 4,100 miles in diameter. The length of its year is 687 days; or, in other words, it completes its revolution round the sun in that space of time. On Mars, spots of a very definite and permanent character have been observed; so much so, that maps or charts have been made, purporting to show the continents and seas. These spots, however, are subject to slight variations at times; but, as Sir John Herschel observes, "the variety in the spots may arise from the planet not being destitute of atmosphere and cloud; and what adds greatly to the probability of this, is the appearance of brilliant white spots at its poles, which have been conjectured, with some probability, to be snow, as they disappear when they have been long exposed to the sun, and are greatest when just emerging from their polar winter, the snow line then extending to about six degrees from the pole."[*]

"The axis of Mars inclines to the plane of its orbit to very nearly the same extent as that of the Earth. It is, therefore, probable that Mars has seasons quite analogous to ours, but of greater length, because the year of Mars is equal to nearly a year and eleven months of

[*] Outlines of Astronomy, p. 570.

our time. The effect of the seasons appears to be very clearly displayed in the white spots of each pole." *

This planet, indeed, possesses many striking and peculiar analogies with our Earth, and had it a moon, would appear very much the same as we might expect our Earth to do, could we see it from Mercury or Venus.

Travelling onwards, at a distance of about 250,000,000 miles from the sun, we encounter, instead of a large planet, a number of small bodies known as the asteroids. According to the general opinion, these bodies are fragments of one large planet, destroyed either by some enormous volcanic agency within, or by collision with a comet. In fact, long before any of these asteroids were discovered, theory suggested the existence of a large planet between Mars and the next planet, Jupiter.

" As early as 1784, Baron de Zach, struck with the remarkable law of Bode, even went so far as to compute the probable distance and period of the now generally suspected planet. The impression that a new world would soon be added to the system, grew deeper and stronger in the minds of astronomers, until finally, in 1800, at a meeting held at Lilienthal by six distinguished observers, the subject was dis-

* Telescopic Teachings, p. 99.

cussed with deep earnestness, and it was finally resolved that the long-suspected, but yet undiscovered world, should be made the object of strict and persevering research. The range of the zodiac was divided into twenty-four parts, and distributed among an equal number of observers, whose duty it was to scrutinise their particular regions, and detect, if possible, any moving body which might show itself among the fixed stars. . . . .

" Piazzi, of Palermo, in Sicily, was one of the planet-searching association. He had already distinguished himself as an eminent and accurate observer, and had with indefatigable zeal constructed a most extensive catalogue of the relative places of the fixed stars, and thus, in some sense, anticipated a part of the labour that the search for the suspected planet contemplated. Assisted by his own and by preceding catalogues, he entered on the great work with the energy and zeal which distinguished all his great astronomical efforts. On the evening of the first day of the year 1801, this astronomer had his attention attracted by a small star in the constellation of the Bull, which he took to be one in the catalogue of Mayer; but, on examination, it was found not to occupy any place either in Mayer's or his own catalogue. Yet it was so small that it was

an easy matter to account for this fact by its
having been overlooked in preceding explo-
rations of the region in which it was found.
With intense anxiety the astronomer awaited
the evening of the following night to settle the
great question whether the newly-detected star
was a fixed or moving body.

" On the evening of the 2nd January, he
repaired to his observatory, and as soon as the
fading twilight permitted, directed the telescope
to the exact point in which, on the preceding
evening, his suspicious star had been located.
The spot was blank ! But another, which was
distant 4' in right ascension, and 3¼' in declina-
tion, at a spot which, on the previous night,
had certainly been vacant, was now gleaming
with the bright little object which, on the preceding evening, had so earnestly fixed his
attention, and for which he was again so
anxiously seeking.   Night after night he
watched its retrograde motion—a motion precisely such as it ought to have—in case it were
the long-desired planet, until, on the 12th, it
became stationary, and then slowly commenced
progressing in the order of the signs.   Piazzi
was unfortunately taken ill, his observations
were suspended, and such was the difficulty of
intercommunication, that although he sent
intelligence of his discovery to Bode and

Orani, associates in the great enterprise, the newly-discovered body was already lost in the rays of the sun, before it became possible to renew the train of observations by which its orbit might be made known. Piazzi feared to announce the newly-discovered body to be the suspected planet. His observations were few, and he was the only person in the world who had seen it. Bode no sooner received the intelligence of its discovery than he at once pronounced it to be the long-sought planet; and from the scanty materials furnished by Piazzi, Olbers, Burkhart, and Gauss, all computed the elements of its orbit, settled the great fact that it was a superior planet, and that its orbit was included between Mars and Jupiter. Some doubt, however, yet rested on the subject, and the disengagement of the planet from the beams of the sun was awaited with the greatest interest."*

Months rolled away in fruitless searching, until at length Gauss, by a long and intricate calculation, determined its position.

"The telescope was directed to the spot, and lo! the beautiful little orb flashed once more on the eager gaze of the youthful astronomer. For one entire year had the planet been sought in vain, and but for the powerful analysis of

* Orbs of Heaven.

Gauss, nothing but years of persevering toil could have wiped away the reproach which rested on astronomy."*

Since that time no less than fifty-five others have been added to the list; and it is more than probable that many more may yet be added, whilst others may continue undiscovered from their smallness.

This brings us to notice Jupiter, a planet of enormous magnitude, being something over 1,300 times larger than our earth. Its diameter is 90,000 miles, and its distance from the sun 485,000,000 miles. The length of its year is 4,333 days, or very nearly twelve of our years, and it performs a revolution on its axis in ten hours.

Jupiter is accompanied by four moons, which were discovered by Galileo only two years after the invention of the telescope. "He was looking through his telescope at Jupiter, at one o'clock in the morning of January 7th, 1610, when he observed three small stars near the body of the planet—two to the east, and one to the west of it. They were all in a straight line, and he thought that they appeared very bright, but he concluded they were fixed stars, which happened to be in the same direction as the planet. He looked again at the planet on

* Orbs of Heaven.

the 8th, without having any particular motive for doing so, that he could afterwards recollect. The little stars were quite differently arranged. All appeared to the west of Jupiter, and nearer to each other than on the preceding night. Now, the philosopher knew that Jupiter, being a planet, was naturally to be expected to change its place among the fixed stars; but Jupiter was, according to all calculations, *moving to the west* at that time, and how could it then be found to the *east* of the three stars? Yet such was the fact.

" Galileo waited for the following night with the utmost anxiety, but was disappointed, for the heavens were wholly veiled in clouds! But in the night of the 10th he saw the planet again. Two only of the stars appeared, both on the east of Jupiter. He now concluded that these stars really moved. On the 11th, he still saw two stars, both to the east of Jupiter, but one of them twice as large as the other, being no doubt quite close to a third satellite. On this night Galileo drew the conclusion, from all he had observed, ' that there were in the heavens three stars, which revolved round Jupiter, in the same manner that Venus and Mercury revolve round the sun.' He observed them again on January 12th, and on the 13th he perceived that the number was four." *

* Martyrs of Science, p. 27.

L

Next to Jupiter is the remarkable planet Saturn, accompanied with eight satellites, and surrounded by a ring. Its distance from the sun is 890,000,000 miles, round which he revolves in twenty-nine years and a-half, and on his own axis in ten hours and a-half. The diameter of Saturn is 79,000 miles. The appearance this planet presents in the telescope is very striking, and if properly observed, divisions may be seen in the ring, which appears composed of three rings, one within the other. Every fifteen years Saturn may be seen apparently without a ring, owing to the ring being perpendicular to the earth's plane; and as the thickness is not so much as a hundred miles, would be perfectly invisible unless to telescopes of extraordinary power. "At such times the satellites of Saturn may be most easily observed. Eight of these satellites have been discovered at very different times, since Saturn was first examined with the telescope." *

"Saturn's sky must be splendid, with eight moons continually changing their places, and with the magnificent rings, which must appear to the *inhabitants* † of those regions which lie above their enlightened sides, as vast arches spanning the sky from horizon to horizon. On the

* Cosmos, vol. iii., p. 386.
† Herschel's Treatise, p. 286.

other hand, in the regions beneath the dark side of the rings, a solar eclipse of fifteen years in duration under their shadow must afford to our ideas an inhospitable asylum to animated beings, ill compensated for by the faint light from the satellites. But we shall do wrong to judge of the fitness, or unfitness, of their condition from what we see around us, when, perhaps, the very combinations which convey to our minds only images of horror, may be in reality theatres of the most striking and glorious displays of beneficent contrivance." *

The next planet in the system is Uranus, and we are now approaching the confines of this vast area, after travelling a space of one thousand eight hundred million miles. Its year, or annual period, is eighty-four years, and the length of its day nine hours and a half. Its diameter is 34,500 miles, and it is attended by eight satellites, six of which were discovered by Sir William Herschell, and the other two, a few years ago, by Mr. Lassell, of Liverpool.†

And now for the last planet in our system —Neptune; a lasting monument, so long as astronomy shall be a science, to those two gigantic minds — Adams and Leverier—who

* Telescopic Teachings, p. 122.
† More Worlds than One, p. 29.

computed with such certainty the whereabouts
of this then unknown and unsuspected world.

It is three thousand millions of miles from
the sun, and forty-two thousand miles in
diameter, and the time of its revolution round
the sun is 60,127 days.

At present there has only been one satellite
of Neptune discovered, although it is more
than probable that there are others; the distance of this satellite from the body of the
planet is computed to be about 250,000
miles, around which it revolves in twenty-five
days and twenty-one hours.

" As early as the 10th of November, 1845,
M. Leverier presented a memoir to the Royal
Academy of Sciences in Paris, in which he
determined the exact perturbations of Jupiter
and Saturn on Uranus.   This was followed by
a memoir, read before the Academy on the first
of June, 1846, in which he demonstrated that
it was impossible to render an exact account
of the perturbations of Uranus in any other
way than by admitting the existence of a *new
planet* exterior to the orbit of Uranus, and
whose heliocentric longitude he fixed at 325°,
on the 1st of January, 1847.   On the 30th of
August, 1846, a third memoir was presented
to the Academy, in which the elements of the
orbit of the unknown planet were fixed,

together with its mass and actual position, with greater accuracy, giving, on the 1st January, 1847, 326° 32', for its heliocentric longitude. Finally, on the 5th of October, 1847, a fourth memoir was read, relative to the determination of the plane of the orbit of the constructive planet." *

And now we turn briefly to notice the researches of our own countryman, Mr. Adams; and it is a singular fact, that, although this gentleman's researches were prior to Leverier's by some two or three years, yet the latter, by some peculiarity or other, generally gets placed first, and receives the greater praise; not that we would rob M. Leverier of one iota of the praise due to him in this gigantic discovery; but " honour to whom honour is due."

" Whatever honour is, therefore, due to M. Leverier — and it is certainly great—equal honour and praise are due to Mr. Adams. The former gentleman has had some rewards for his labours; we believe that the latter gentleman's honours are yet to come. . . . It was stated by Professor Challis, of Cambridge, that Mr. Adams, Fellow of St. John's College, showed him a memorandum, made in the year 1841, recording his intention of attempting to solve the problem arising out of

* The Orbs of Heaven, p. 189.

the perturbations of Uranus, as soon as he had
taken his B.A. degree. Accordingly, after
graduating, in 1843, he obtained an approxi-
mate solution, and afterwards pursued the
subject to that extent, as actually to place in
the hands of the Astronomer Royal, and of
Professor Challis, the elements of the then
unknown planet, before any elements of this
planet had been obtained, or at least published,
by M. Leverier."*

To our minds, the discovery of the planet
Neptune is one of the—if not *the*—greatest
achievements of the human mind, and certainly
the greatest warrant on record for the truth of
astronomy, and the uniformity of the laws
which govern the universe. Here are two
men, both totally unknown to each other, at
almost the same time, computing and deter-
mining, not only the distance and orbit of an
unknown world, but, with their gigantic intel-
lects, actually telling the size and weight of
that which few would have dared to say existed,
and which even they themselves had not seen.
And now we take our leave of the more sub-
stantial objects connected with the solar system,
to notice those peculiar bodies which sometimes startle us with their brilliancy, and
known as comets. Interesting, indeed, are the

* The Orbs of Heaven.

accounts of the appearance of these bodies in the early ages of the world's history, and strange and wild have been the traditions and superstitions connected with their appearance; but, interesting as these accounts are, it is not in our province to notice them here; our object is simply to give a description of their characteristics in connexion with the solar system. The usual appearance of a comet consists of a "nucleus," or head, more or less bright, though indistinct in outline, environed by a faint, cloudy atmosphere, and attended by a still fainter, cloudy appearance, called the "tail," extending linearly often through an immense space. The comet of April, 1854, and the remarkable comet of 1858 (Donati's), exemplify this description. Some few comets have, however, appeared, "divested of a tail; and others have been observed with no trace of nucleus." *

" Previous to the discovery of the law of universal gravitation, comets were looked upon as anomalous bodies, of whose motions it was quite impossible to take any account. By some philosophers they were regarded as meteors kindled into a blaze in the earth's atmosphere, and, whenever extinguished, they were lost for ever. Others looked upon them

* Nichol's Cyclopædia, p. 132.

as permanent bodies, revolving in orbits far
above the moon, and re-appearing at the end of
long but certain intervals. When, however, it
was discovered that, under the influence of
gravitation, any revolving world might describe
either of the four curves, the circle, ellipse,
parabola, or hyperbola, it at once became
manifest that the eccentric movements of the
comets might be perfectly represented by
giving to them orbits of the parabolic or
hyperbolic form—the sun being located in the
focus of the curve. According to this theory,
the comet would become visible in its approach
to its perihelion, or nearest distance from the
sun—would here blaze with uncommon splendour, and, in its recess to the remote parts of
its orbit, would gradually fade from the sight,
relaxing its speed, and performing a large proportion of its vast curve far beyond the reach
of human vision." *

This is precisely what takes place, and such
are the fair deductions from the great and
universal law, which the time-honoured and
immortal Newton has revealed to the world.
As to the physical or cosmical constitution of
these bodies, little, indeed, is known; and
numberless almost have been the theories set
forth concerning them; few of which, however,

* The Orbs of Heaven, p. 150.

approach, much less adequately meet, an explanation of the various phenomena which, from time to time, have been observed. Whether they are gaseous, electric, or composed of matter in a brilliant state of incandescence, or whether they are the whole three combined, it is impossible to speak with any degree of certainty, but we have our own opinion concerning them. Why may they not be bodies possessing a solid nucleus, in a state of the most extreme magnetic or electric tension? And, unless we are much mistaken, the whole of the phenomena observed in these bodies may be explained by this theory. Take, for instance, the excessively rarified appearance of the " coma," or tail. Do we not find a great analogy existing between this and the brilliant, though attenuated, appearance of the passage of an electric current through extremely rarefied air? Every student of electricity must be acquainted with the peculiar nature of this light; and if a small jet of gas-light be seen through it, it will positively appear to render the jet more brilliant instead of obscuring it; we notice this fact in connexion with the transit of the beautiful comet of 1858 across Arcturus, on which occasion that star was seen through the densest part of the tail; and although we have no delicate photometer to measure the degree of light, yet by many astronomers Arcturus was thought to shine with greater brilliancy during the transit.

By this theory also may be explained the cause why the tails of comets are turned from the sun, by simply supposing them to be in the same electrical condition as the sun's atmosphere, which would cause the ray emanating from the nucleus to be repelled or turned in an opposite direction. In this way also may be explained why the magnitude of the tail increases as it nears the sun, as, of course, the nearer the comet approaches, the greater the repulsion must be, and consequently increases the intensity of the electric induction, thereby causing the extension of the electro-luminous ray, precisely similar— only on an infinitely greater scale—to the ray emanating from the conductor of an electric machine. It will be impossible, however, under the present circumstances, to follow out this theory to any greater extent, as it might form the subject of a book of itself; but sufficient has been set forth to show the plausibility of such a theory. We have now described all the permanent objects visible in the solar system, but before finally quitting the subject, we shall briefly notice those peculiar bodies, " meteors," or what are vulgarly known as shooting stars; these bodies are so common, that they may be seen on any fine star-light night, by anybody who will take the trouble to look for them. There is but little doubt that they are common to the whole solar system, and perform their revolutions round the sun in orbits similar to the planets, only becoming visible to us when passing through the denser parts of the earth's atmosphere. On certain nights during the year, however, they may be seen in great numbers, especially about the 10th to the 12th of August, and the 12th of November.

" The theory proposed to account for these periodical visits of the shooting stars is, that a belt of them is situated somewhere within the limits of the solar system, revolves round the sun, and cuts through that portion of the earth's orbit which our planet must occupy on those particular nights in August and November."*

" Thus far our attention has been directed to an examination of the achievements of the human mind within the limits of our own peculiar system. We have swept outward from the sun through the planetary worlds, until we have reached the frontier limits of this mighty family. Standing upon the latest found of all

* Telescopic Teachings, p. 169.

the planets, at a distance of more than 3,000,000,000 of miles from the sun, we are able to look backwards, and examine the worlds and systems which are all embraced within the vast circumference of Neptune's orbit. An occasional comet, overleaping this mighty boundary, and flying swiftly past us, buries itself in the mighty abyss of space, to return, after its 'long journey of a thousand years,' and report to the inhabitants of earth the influences which have swayed its movements in the invisible regions whither it speeds its flight."*

And, after all, this vast system is but an infinitesimally small portion of the universe; it is but as one grain of sand from the sea-shore, or one drop of water from the mighty ocean, "one unit among the unnumbered millions which fill the crowded regions of space." Could we leave our world and travel to the distance of the nearest fixed star, our sun would not be distinguished from the other stars; it would appear only as a small diamond point, equal in apparent size to a star of the second magnitude. Is it not fair, then, for us to suppose that all these sparkling orbs are suns like ours, with their systems of planets, comets, and meteors? And when we consider how many thousands of these are visible to the unassisted eye, and how in-

* Orbs of Heaven, p. 171.

numerably more are visible with the assistance
of the telescope, how infinitely small is this
world of ours when compared with this grand
array? But, stop, we are drawing our com-
parisons too soon, for we are only on the
borders of the infinite at present. Look for a
moment at that filmy belt of light, " the milky
way," and the various hazy nebulæ which are
scarcely perceptible to the unassisted eye ;—
direct the telescope thither, and this filmy haze
for the most part is resolvable into distinct
although minute specks of light ! How
astounding ! Each of these specks is a sun, a
glorious sun, a sun perhaps hundreds of times
larger and more magnificent than our own.
Standing here we again glance backwards,—
our sun is lost in obscurity, its light is too
feeble to reach us. " All behind blazes with
the light of countless orbs, scattered in wild
magnificence, while all before us is deep, im-
penetrable, unbroken darkness. No glance of
human vision can pierce the dark profound.
But summoning the telescope to our aid, let
us pursue our mighty journey through space ;
for in the distance we are just able to discover
a faint haze of light, a minute luminous cloud
which comes up to meet us, and towards this
object we will urge our flight. We leave the
shining millions of our own great cluster far

behind. Its stars are shrinking and fading ; its dimensions are contracting. It once filled the whole heavens, and now its myriads of blazing orbs could almost be grasped with a single hand.

"But now look forward. A new universe of astonishing grandeur bursts on the sight. The cloud of light has swelled and expanded, and its millions of suns now fill the whole heavens. . . . . . Such examinations absolutely overwhelm the mind, and the wild dream of the German poet becomes a sort of sublime reality :*—God called up from dreams a man in the vestibule of heaven, saying, ' Come thou hither, and see the glory of my house.' And to the servants that stood around His throne He said, ' Take him and undress him from his robes of flesh ; cleanse his vision, and put a new breath into his nostrils ; only touch not with any change his human heart—the heart that weeps and trembles.' It was done : and with a mighty angel for his guide, the man stood ready for his infinite voyage ; and from the terraces of heaven, without sound or farewell, at once they wheeled away into endless space. Sometimes with the solemn flight of angel wing they fled through Zaarahs of darkness, through wildernesses of death, that

* Orbs of Heaven.

divided the worlds of light; sometimes they swept over frontiers, that were quickening under prophetic motions from God. Then, from a distance that is counted only in heaven, light dawned for a time through a sleepy film; by unutterable pace the light swept to *them*; they, by unutterable pace, to the light. In a moment the rushing of planets was upon them; in a moment, the blazing of suns was around them.

"Then came eternities of twilight, that revealed but were not revealed. On the right hand and on the left, towered mighty constellations, that, by self-repetitions and answers from afar, that, by counterpositions, built up triumphal gates, whose architraves, whose archways, horizontal, upright, rested, rose, at altitudes by spans that seemed ghostly from infinitude. Without measure were the architraves, past number the archways, beyond memory the gates. Within were stairs that scaled eternities below; above was below, below was above, to the man stripped of gravitating body: depth was swallowed up in height insurmountable—height was swallowed up in depth unfathomable. Suddenly, as thus they rode from infinite to infinite,— suddenly, as thus they tilted over abysmal worlds—a mighty cry arose, that systems more mysterious, that worlds more billowy, other heights and other depths, were coming, were nearing, were at hand.

"Then, the man sighed and stopped, shuddered and wept.   His overladened heart uttered itself in tears ; and he said, 'Angel, I will go no farther; for the spirit of man acheth with this infinity.   Insufferable is the glory of God.   Let me lie down in the grave, and hide me from the persecution of the infinite, for end, I see, there is none.'   And from all the listening stars that shone around issued a choral voice,   'The man speaks truly; end there is none, that ever yet we heard of.' 'End is there none?' the angel solemnly demanded: 'Is there indeed no end? and is this the sorrow that kills you?'   But no voice answered, that he might answer himself. Then the angel threw up his glorious hands to the heaven of heavens, saying, 'End is there none, to the universe of God.   Lo! also, there is no beginning.'"

ESSAY VII.

ON THE MULTIPLICITY OF WORLDS.

FITNESS OF THE SUN FOR HABITATION—THE MOON, IS IT
INHABITED—THE USEFULNESS OF THE SUN AND MOON,
AN ARGUMENT AGAINST THEIR HABITATION—ANA-
LOGIES BETWEEN THE EARTH AND THE OTHER PLANETS—
OBJECTIONS ANSWERED—SATURNIAN SYSTEM—INSIG-
NIFICANCE OF THE EARTH—UNIVERSALITY OF LIFE—AGE
OF THE EARTH—NATURAL ECONOMY IN CREATION—
OTHER WORLDS, BIBLICALLY CONSIDERED—SCIENTIFIC
REVELATIONS NOT ANTAGONISTIC TO SCRIPTURE—
GALILEO AND THE CHURCH OF ROME—NECESSITY FOR
MORAL EVIL—RESTITUTION OF ALL THINGS—MAN'S
FUTURE HOME IN THE UNIVERSE.

Ask for what end the heavenly bodies shine,
Earth for whose use? Pride answers, " 'Tis for mine:
Seas roll to waft me, suns to light me rise,
My footstool earth, my canopy the skies."—POPE.

THE probability as to whether the heavenly
bodies are inhabited, is a subject which has
excited great interest for a considerable time,
and which has also provoked, at different

M

intervals, a great deal of contention among the philosophical and investigating community; those on the one hand who believe in a plurality of worlds, and on the other, those who regard the heavenly bodies as being no more than huge masses of lifeless matter. We therefore devote this essay to the investigation of the various arguments used for and against, we at the same time believing in the existence of other inhabited worlds.

Perhaps the least likely place which might be supposed, by ordinary thinking minds, to be fit for habitation would be the sun; and, really, in attempting to show the probability of its being inhabited, there is a great deal to contend against in the not altogether unnatural popular errors which are likely to beset the mind. In the first place, people might argue that if the light emanating from the sun be so intense—at times, even here, at the distance of 95,000,000 of miles—that the human eye cannot bear the excessive brightness, what must it be on the body of the sun itself? And then, again, if the heat of its beams at this enormous distance be so great, what must be the intensity on its surface? Take only a small lens and concentrate a few of its rays, and see the result; bring any combustible substance in the focus and it is immediately ignited.

This little experiment will serve to give some idea of the excessive heat which must be raging there. And it will be no great stretch of the imagination to suppose that any one might justly demand, How is it possible that any living creature could exist there, however salamander-like they might be?

By such questions as these we are met with at the onset; and however conclusive at first sight they may appear, still we hope we shall not only be able to contend against them in support of our argument, but offer such explanations as shall adequately meet all the objections which may be raised against the fitness of the sun for habitation. And, in the consideration of this subject, let it be perfectly understood, that however probable, after our explanation, it may appear that there *are* inhabitants of some sort or other in the sun,— still, let us not forget that of all the heavenly bodies, the sun possesses the least analogy with our earth, and nothing in common with this earth and the other planets; so we have no support here by parity of reasoning.

And now for the two great and principal objections to this hypothesis—the excessive light and heat to which the inhabitants of the sun must necessarily be exposed. That this excess of light and heat exists there, cannot for a moment be doubted; but it is for us to consider under what circumstances. The sun is an opaque, dark body, surrounded by a luminous atmosphere; between this luminous atmosphere, however, and the body of the sun, also exists one or probably two other atmospheres. And we do not state this from mere supposition, for on closely examining the spots which are constantly making their appearance on the surface of the sun, we find them to be of different shades, the centres being much darker than the edges; this may be readily accounted for by supposing that on the surface of the sun there is an atmosphere precisely similar to our own, although it may be more loaded with clouds, and that between this and the luminous atmosphere there is one of far greater density. This will account for the different shades observed in the solar spots; and furthermore will show, in the most satisfactory manner possible, how the light and heat from the outer atmosphere may be subdued by the density of the inner one, and thus render the surface of the sun fit for life of as great or greater delicacy as exists on this world of ours.

According to some photometrical experiments by Sir William Herschell, it was estimated that the body of the sun only received the seven-thousandth part of the light and heat of the incandescent atmosphere.

Another objection which has been raised against the sun being inhabited, is its great specific gravity, which is thirty times that of our earth; therefore, could a man of ordinary weight be transported to the surface of the sun he would there weigh nearly two tons, and would be crushed by his own weight. But this kind of arguing is only skin-deep after all, for it is absurd to suppose any other than that the specific gravity of the air will be proportionately greater; and that being the case, would support exactly the same kind of life as exists here. But we are not bound to admit that it is inhabited by beings like ourselves.; indeed, it would appear as though the sun was peculiarly constituted for the existence of the highest order of beings; for, apart from its gigantic size, and being the very centre of the system, it rejoices in the possession of uninterrupted day, "for there is no night there," no icy blasts or chilling snows there, perpetual spring in radiance reigns and clothes the hills with living green. There, arrayed in eternal sunshine, may exist seraphic beings who may not have been made "a little lower than the angels," but who are now rejoicing, it may be, in elysiums of unchequered bliss. This state of things would hardly do for us poor sons of toil; we require night, that we may rest from our weariness and labour. But, glory be to God, this is only our transition state, our pilgrimage to that which shall far surpass all our most exalted conceptions. " But as it is written, Eye hath not seen, nor ear heard, neither have entered into the heart of man, the things which God hath prepared for them that love Him."* Thus have we endeavoured to show and explain how it is not only possible but probable that even the sun is inhabited. And, however antagonistic it may be to some peoples' minds, or however inexplicable it may appear, still it may be none the less true.

And if we turn to notice the planets, we have a vast field open for investigation and inquiry. We have, in many of these, to consider worlds in every respect similar to our own, scarcely one inferior to ours, and some of such magnificence and grandeur as to make this world dwindle down into almost insignificance, and remind us what a small place we occupy in the vast infinity of the universe of God. Turn we first, however, to notice our nearest neighbour in space, the moon. Seen through a telescope, the surface presents the appearance of mountain and valley, hill and dale, precisely

* 1 Cor. ii. 9.

as we might reasonably expect our earth to appear, could we view it under similar circumstances; but here, again, we find how difficult it is

"To see ourselves as others see us!"

Now, then, let us suppose for a moment that we know for a certainty that the moon *is* inhabited, should we not consider it very ridiculous for the people who inhabit the moon to suppose that this world was only made to light their path by night, as it really does; for be it known, that our world would appear to the inhabitants of the moon very similar as the moon does to us—with this difference, that it would be eight times the apparent size; it would rise and set, and go through all the various phases, in the same way as the moon appears to us—in fact, the one may be taken as the model of the other.

Sir William Herschell, speaking of the probability of the moon being inhabited, says— " Its situation, with respect to the sun, is much like that of the earth, and by a rotation on its axis it enjoys an agreeable variety of seasons, and of day and night. To the moon, our globe will appear to be a very capital satellite, undergoing the same regular changes of illumination as the moon does to the earth. The sun, the planets, and the starry constellations of the heavens, will rise and set there as they do here, and heavy bodies will fall on the moon as they do on the earth. *There seems only to be wanting, in order to complete the analogy, that it should be inhabited like the earth.*"

By many, however, it has been supposed that the moon is void of atmosphere: could this supposition be established, it would at once put an end to the idea of its being inhabited—but this stupid theory is fortunately dying out.   We believe in the universality of the atmosphere throughout the solar system, and this atmosphere is subject to the law of gravitation, and that its density varies in proportion to the specific gravity of the planet which it surrounds.   We cannot well see how matter can exist without an atmosphere; but to suppose there is no atmosphere in the moon is simply absurd, when we see such abundant traces of its existence in the lunar mountains: the craters testify to the great volcanic action, and this, as everybody knows, is caused by the expansion and explosion of gases; besides this, there is combustion.   This must be supported by the most important constituent in our atmosphere—*i e.*, oxygen.   Therefore we are bound to admit that the moon, in common with this world, has an atmosphere, and therefore capable of supporting inhabitants.   However, be this

as it may, it is by no means necessary that
those who believe in a plurality of worlds
within the limits of our own system, should
adopt the opinion that the sun which lights it,
and the many satellites which light the primary planets, should be inhabited worlds.

They form an entirely different class of
bodies, and the arguments employed to show
that they may be inhabited, are of a different
nature from those analogies which so strongly
apply to the primary planets. The sun has a
great function to perform in controlling the
movements of the whole system. It is the
mainspring of the great planetary chronome-
ters, without which they would stop, and rush
into destructive collision. It is the lamp which
yields them the light, without which life would
perish. It is the furnace which supplies the
fuel, without which organic nature would be
destroyed. Created for such noble purposes,
we are led by no analogy to assign to it an
additional function. The very same remark
may be applied to our moon, and to all the
satellites of the system. They are the domestic
lamps which light the primary planets in the
absence of the sun; and all of them, as well as
our own, may exercise the other office of producing the tides of their oceans. It is quite
otherwise with the primary planets: they have

no conceivable function to perform but that of supporting inhabitants, unless we give them the additional one, which they are all fit for performing, and which they perform so well, of becoming gigantic lamps to their satellites; and if we invest them with this function, we obtain an argument for the satellites themselves being inhabited." *

But what shall we then say respecting the planets which are without moons? They cannot have been created in vain; yet, if they are uninhabited, they most certainly are vain and useless; for tell me not that those myriad sparkling orbs were created merely for man to look at—we say it is downright presumption to suppose such a thing for a moment.

This brings us to the consideration of the planets; and it is with much greater satisfaction and confidence that we shall attempt to argue in favour of their being inhabited, than we did in the consideration of the sun and moon. The two inferior planets, Mercury and Venus, will first occupy our attention, for, next the moon, they are our nearest neighbours, and in them we find many peculiar and striking analogies to our earth.

Mercury is only about half the size of the earth, while Venus is about equal in size to

* More Worlds than One, p. 98.

the earth. Both these worlds—for so we will call them—have a day of almost exactly the same duration as our own. Mercury's year is rather short, it is true, but that would be no drawback to the inhabitants; while the year of Venus is about two-thirds of our own, which, in some cases, perhaps, might be deemed an advantage. An attempt has been made, in objection to these two planets being inhabited, to prove that the light would be far too intense for the sight, and would very quickly bring on blindness; but a less sensitive retina, or a smaller pupil, would be all that is required to obviate this.

The planet Mars, the first superior planet, is also only about half the size of our earth; its year is very nearly equal to two of ours, and the length of its day a trifle more than our own. Mars is really a beautiful object in the telescope, by means of which we can see its continents and oceans, its snow-crowned poles, and even detect clouds floating in its atmosphere; in fact, it appears as a beautiful little miniature world. Unlike our world only in one respect, which is, it has no moon; however, "the numerous analogies which we have indicated, give the highest degree of probability, not to say moral certainty, to the conclusion that the three planets, Mars, Venus, and

Mercury, which, with the earth, revolve nearest to the sun, are, like the earth, appropriated by the omnipotent Creator and Ruler of the universe to races very closely resembling, if not absolutely identical with those by which the earth is peopled."*

Passing by the planetoids, or asteroids, which no analogy will warrant us in believing to be inhabited, we have the planet Jupiter, the largest of all the planets, being over one thousand three hundred times greater than the earth, and is attended—as we have before observed—with four moons. What a beautiful appearance must the heavens present to the inhabitants of this planet! Imagine, if you can, four beautiful moons, in all their various phases, in the heavens at one time; our single moon we consider beautiful enough, but what the appearance of four at a time would be, we can have but very faint ideas.

The shortness of Jupiter's day has been thought by some sufficient grounds for rejecting the idea of its being inhabited; but as the day and night are equally divided, the rest of the one half must surely be sufficient to compensate for the labour of the other.

Another objection has been the distance of

* Dr. Lardner's "Museum of Science and Art," vol. i., p. 23.

Jupiter from the sun, and the consequent loss of light and heat would be so great as to be incapable of sustaining either animal or vegetable life, and that all its oceans and seas would be huge fields of ice. But in meeting this difficulty, which seems, at first sight, to assume a serious character, we shall be able to explain another which has been thought almost conclusive.

We must not suppose that the planets are entirely dependent upon the sun for heat; there are other causes equally efficacious in producing warmth, *i.e.*, heat, which may be contained in the bowels of the planet, and the heat which may be developed by the density of its atmosphere. If we assume this latter theory, then are we able to explain how the enormous specific gravity of the planet Jupiter may be counteracted, by the support given by so dense an atmosphere. And the same argument that we applied to the possibility of the sun being inhabited, will apply with equal power to Jupiter, or any of the other planets.

Is it right, think you, for us to suppose that this beautiful planet has been created for naught, and that its moons have been shining night after night, and illuminating its landscapes, and clothing them as with a mantle of silver, and no one there to appreciate its beauties? No! we reject the idea as monstrous and untenable, only to be indulged in by the most ignorant, presuming, and narrow-minded.

One singularity not yet noticed with regard to Jupiter, is the uniformity of its climate.

" The axis of Jupiter is inclined to the plane of its orbit, at the very small angle of 3° 5′ 30″, while that of the earth, as is well known, has an inclination of 23° 28′ 30″. As this inclination limits the temperature of the seasons, the extent of the zones and the varieties of the climates, it follows, that in Jupiter these phenomena must be very different from those of the earth. The extreme variation of the altitude of the sun at noon does not much exceed six degrees in any latitude; a change which cannot produce any very sensible variation in the temperature of the seasons. On this planet there is, therefore, perpetual spring. The tropics of Jupiter are only three degrees north and south of his equator, and the polar circles, which include the only parts of the planet at which the sun remains at any time below or above the horizon, during a complete revolution, are limited to three degrees around the poles.

" In fine, the diurnal phenomena in Jupiter are, at all times, nearly the same as they are upon the earth at the equinoxes." *

* Dr. Lardner's "Museum of Science and Art," i., 34.

And now, taking our leave of Jupiter, our leviathan planet, the study of which, we trust, has afforded a well-merited interest, we have to notice the planet Saturn; and perhaps, of all the planets, the most interesting, especially to an astronomical observer, will be this; for although in point of size it is far less significant than Jupiter, yet it is a stupendous orb, being nearly 900 times greater than our earth; and surrounded as it is by its beautiful belts, and as many moons as there are primary planets in the system, it cannot fail to take its rank the first amidst the planetary bodies.

Saturn, as seen in the telescope, presents an appearance little inferior to Jupiter; for although its disc is very much smaller, yet, with its rings, it is really a magnificent object.

On this planet, as on Jupiter, have been observed belts or bands running across its disc in a direction parallel to its equator. These, seen with a telescope of good magnifying power, prove to be openings in the clouds, which, in this planet and Jupiter, are so dense. The cause of these belts arises from what we term "trade winds," which distribute the clouds in bands or streaks parallel with the equator; and the causes of these atmospheric currents arise, first, from the velocity of the planet on its axis, and next, by the action of the solar heat upon the atmosphere within the immediate vicinity of the equator. It therefore follows, that the greater the velocity of the planet, the stronger and more decided will these atmospheric currents be. Now, this is exactly the result with both Jupiter and Saturn; for while these planets are performing five revolutions, the earth will only have completed two.

" It may, therefore, be inferred that the prevalence of atmospheric currents on these planets parallel to their equators, is far more constant and more strong than upon the earth; and since the masses of cloud with which they are loaded are greater and more permanent, the effects of such currents upon their distribution in equatorial strata or bands, must be supposed to be far more conspicuous."*

Our remarks as to the habitability of Jupiter will apply with equal force to Saturn, with this difference—that while Jupiter has but four moons, Saturn has eight; and besides this, the beautiful rings, which must appear to the inhabitants of " those regions which lie above their enlightened sides, as vast arches spanning the sky from horizon to horizon."†

" On the other hand," as Sir John Herschel

* Dr. Lardner's " Museum of Science and Art," i. 37.
† Herschel's " Treatise, " p. 286.

continues, " in the regions beneath the dark side of the rings, a solar eclipse of fifteen years in duration under their shadow must afford to our ideas an inhospitable asylum to animated beings, ill compensated by the faint light of the satellites. But we shall do wrong to judge of the fitness or unfitness of their condition from what we see around us, when, perhaps, the very combinations which convey to our minds only images of horror, may be in reality theatres of the most striking and glorious displays of beneficent contrivance."

Other writers on this subject, however, ignore this fact ; and Dr. Lardner, in a memoir read before the Astronomical Society in 1853, clearly " demonstrated that the infinite skill of the great Architect of the universe has not permitted that this stupendous annular appendage, the uses of which still remain undiscovered, should be the cause of such darkness and desolation to the inhabitants of the planet, and such an aggravation of the rigours of their fifteen years' winter, as it has been inferred to be from the reasoning of the eminent astronomers already named, as well as many others, who have either adopted their conclusions, or arrived at like inferences by other arguments. It is shown on the contrary that by the apparent motion of the heavens, produced by the

N

diurnal rotation of Saturn, the celestial objects, including, of course, the sun and the eight moons, are not carried parallel to the edges of the rings, as has been hitherto supposed; that they are moved so as to pass alternately from side to side of each of these edges; that, in general, such objects as pass under the rings are only occulted by them for short intervals before and after their meridional culmination; that, although under some rare and exceptional circumstances and conditions, certain objects, the sun being among the number, are occulted from rising to setting, the continuance of such phenomena is not such as has been supposed, and the places of its occurrence are far more limited.   In short, it has no such character as would deprive the planet of any essential condition of habitability." *

In the consideration, however, of the probability of these planets being inhabited, it will be well to regard the subject in as many different lights as possible.   Let us suppose, for instance, that all the planets, inclusive of our earth, had but just been called into existence by the Omnipotent Creator; which, think you, according to all human reasoning, would have been selected for habitation?   Would it have been our unpretending little earth, or would

* Dr. Lardner's "Museum of Science and Art," vol. i., p. 59.

it have been the gigantic planet Jupiter with its four attendant moons? Shall Uranus with its six moons, or Saturn with its glorious belt and eight attendant moons be rejected; and shall this comparatively insignificant world be peopled? or shall the least amidst creation be inhabited, and shall not the greatest? Our earth neither occupies the nearest, the most central, or the most distant place with regard to the sun and the solar system; it is neither the largest or the most magnificent; in short, there are no attributes connected with it which would warrant us in placing it first in creation; that being the case, we are bound to admit that as one of the least—*i. e.*, our earth—is inhabited, the others, almost to a certainty, must be inhabited also. This is genuine philosophy. Are they not all made by the same divine hand—the same omnipotent Creator?—and all made, doubtless, for a like object, which is, to be inhabited by beings who shall appreciate all their various glories, and give praise to Him who overruleth all things.

"In the two remote planets, Uranus and Neptune, the principal point of analogy with our earth is, that they are lighted with moons—Uranus with six, and Neptune with one, or, perhaps, two; though we have no doubt that, like the other distant planets, he will be found

N 2

to possess a greater number. The power of our best telescopes has not enabled astronomers to discover belts and clouds upon these two planets, and thus determine their daily motion. The oblate form of their discs, too, remains to be discovered; but notwithstanding the absence of these points of analogy, the very existence of such large globes of matter revolving round the sun, and lighted up with moons, cannot fail to satisfy the unprejudiced and inquiring mind that they must have been created for some grand purpose, worthy of their Maker. In the present state of our knowledge, it is impossible to conceive any other purpose than that of being the residence of animal and intellectual life.

" There is one consideration in reference to the two remote planets, Uranus and Neptune, which some of our readers may regard as adding to the probability of their being worlds like our own. Some writers, or rather one, for we know of only one, have asserted, ' however destitute planets, moons, and rings may be of inhabitants, they are at least vast scenes of God's presence, and of the activity with which He carries into effect everywhere the laws of nature; and that the glory of creation arises from its being not only the product, but the constant field of God's activity and thought, wisdom and power."* "We shall not venture to ascertain how much more of God's glory is seen in the material structure of Saturn and his ring, and of Jupiter and his satellites, than it is in the minutest insect that lives but for an hour; nor shall we compare gigantic masses of self-luminous or opaque illuminated matter with the smaller organisms which are daily presented to us. We shall admit that the vulgar eye, even, is delighted with the sight of planets made gorgeous by the telescope, that astronomers are entranced by the study of their movements and their perturbations, and that the useful art of navigation may derive some advantage from the eclipses of Jupiter's satellites. The poet, too, may rejoice in ' the soft and tender beauty of the moon,' and in the inspiration of the morning and the evening star. But where is the grandeur, where the utility, where the beauty, where the poetry of the two almost invisible stars which usurp the celestial names of Uranus and Neptune, and which have been seen by none but a very few even of the cultivators of astronomy. The grand discoveries of Kepler, Newton, and La Place were made before these planets were known. They have, therefore, been of no use in establishing the physical laws of the

* " Of the Plurality of Worlds," an Essay, p. 254.

universe.   The seaman in the trackless ocean
never seeks their guidance; to him they have
not even the value of the polar star.   They
contribute nothing to the arts of terrestrial
life; they neither light the traveller on his
journey, nor mark by their feeble ray the happy
hours which are consecrated to friendship and
to love.   They must, therefore, have been
created for other and nobler ends : to be the
abodes of life and intelligence, the colossal
temples where their Creator is recognised and
worshipped; the remotest watch-towers of our
system, from which His works may be better
studied, and His distant glories more readily
descried."*   Here we must pause, in recon-
sidering the subject; we have reached the confines of our system, we have met each difficulty
as it arose in our outward journey from the
sun, and endeavoured to dissipate the mists of
popular and erroneous impressions.   The objections have been great, the difficulties many,
yet we trust they have been satisfactorily
surmounted, and that our explanations will
adequately meet all and every objection.   We
have seen how the Great Ruler of the universe,
who has placed us on this earth, could have
peopled the sun and the moon with like inhabitants, did he but see fit; we have seen how

* More Worlds than One, p. 80.

planet after planet, which we have brought under consideration, has been found suitable for all the various forms of life with which we are acquainted; and how many more varieties of life may exist in those worlds, which we know nothing of. The almost infinite variety in the forms of life, even in our own world, and under our own observation, is wondrously surprising. Need we tell you how peculiarly adapted are various animals for the peculiarities under which they exist? Will you accompany us to the barren wastes of Egypt, and there see how the untiring camel is provided for?—how across those dry and sand-bound plains its thirst is provided for? Or, will you come and see how the tall and handsome giraffe feeds? Will you go and study the fur-clad animals of the poles, or seek the volubility of the tropics? Wherever we go, we shall always find the greatest symmetry prevail; and no matter where we look, we shall always find life. Each drop of water is a world in itself, and the very dust beneath our feet is crowded with life; we scarce can move or breathe without wholesale destruction of life of some kind or other taking place. And shall a drop of water be inhabited with its myriad animalculæ, and shall the stupendous orbs which nightly deck our skies be void? It must not be; it cannot be!

Matter without life seems incredible, and a planet without inhabitants is like a town without inhabitants, only on a larger scale; it is like ships without sailors, or railway trains running to and fro without passengers. And we must insist on universal life and universal matter.

And now we start afresh. Dare we venture further? Shall we pass the confines of our system? Yes, we dare. Onward, must be the cry. We must leave Jupiter, and Saturn, and Neptune far behind, and travel onward until our sun no longer holds a conspicuous place in the heavens, and here we may rest and surmise again. We summon the telescope to our aid, and turn it alike to our sun and the other so-called fixed stars, and what is the result? It is as might be expected: there is no difference discernible. And now, what does this teach us? Does it not tell us, and with greater force than any words could utter, that all those sparkling orbs which fill the heavens with their magnificence, are all suns like our own, centres of other systems of planets, it may be, far more glorious and far more mysterious than our own; that Orion's gorgeous belt may only be the centre of systems still more gorgeous and profound?

"But, surely," we imagine we hear some saying,

" you are not going to tell us that these also are inhabited worlds? You have no analogy which will warrant you in supposing anything of the kind." But stop, do not go too far. You are wrong, as we will now endeavour to explain.

Assuming, in the first place, that each fixed star is a sun, are we not bound by analogy to suppose it to be, like our own, the centre of a planetary system? We can arrive at no other conclusion. Well, then, that being the case, will not analogy point at least to one of the planets of each system as being like our earth, inhabited; and then, adopting the same kind of reasoning as we have with regard to our own system, we obtain the great probability of each individual planet of every system being inhabited, and that they are, in common with our own, governed by the same universal laws.

In further considering this subject, it must occur to all, that, although numbers believe in the general theory, *it* may be regarded and accepted in many different lights. We can easily understand that some will altogether ignore the *possibility* of there being inhabitants in the sun and moon, but who will readily admit the great probability of there being inhabitants in the planets, and in far-off worlds revolving round other suns. While others will confine their belief to our own system, they have no difficulty in believing the whole of *our* planetary system to be the seat of life, but will not extend their belief beyond.   They do not realise the fact that every star in the canopy of heaven is in reality a sun, and the centre of other planetary systems, and that each filmy nebula is a stupendous cluster of suns.   We must admit that the idea is overwhelming, and the vastness is past the comprehension of the finite mind of man, whether they be centres of inhabited worlds or no.

Go out on any fine starlight night, and look upwards at that band of nebulous light—the milky way—what think you of this gorgeous cincture, spreading as a filmy cloud across the entire vault? Can it be possible that it is composed of brilliant stars, but so far removed as only to appear as luminous dust? It is so ; and it has been calculated that, in the sky so occupied, the moon would eclipse over two thousand such stars at once.

Many people, not believing in more worlds than our own, have adopted the singular but ingenious hypothesis of La Place, although at variance at once with Scripture and common sense. He supposes the sun to have been first created with an atmosphere in a state of incandescence, extending beyond the orbits of all the planets, and that one planet after another was formed by the cooling and contracting of the incandescent matter.

But we do not see, even admitting this theory, that there is anything antagonistic to *our* theory. On the contrary, it may even be said to go in our favour, for inasmuch as Neptune would have been formed first, it is only right to suppose it would have been the first to be inhabited. More recently, however, the theory of La Place has been carried to a far greater extent. "The universe is supposed to be filled with *fire mist*, or *star dust*, as it has been called—something like a mixture of smoke and steam. From some unknown cause, two particles attract one another, and are then surrounded by others, which become an infant sun, wriggling itself into motion, increasing in size, and carrying round with it the whole mass of fire mist within the orbit of Neptune, and then forming planets and satellites, as in the last hypothesis. Here, as before, the direct creative power of the Almighty is required to generate the fire mist; but when this is done, His arm is paralysed, and the solar system is manufactured by secondary causes." *

One writer on this subject employs this theory to prove that Mercury and Venus cannot be inhabited, as they are not yet free from this

* More Worlds than One, p. 122.

fire mist; and furthermore, that Jupiter, Saturn, Uranus, and Neptune have no inhabitants, as they are only "immense clouds," or "water and vapour packed into rotating masses," and "driven into the outer parts of the system, or retained there by the central heat of the sun."

It seems to us very remarkable that our earth should be the only place where this fire mist, or star dust, should have so condensed.   The asteroids the same writer regards as "mere shreds and specks of planetary matter;" or as "watery globes, with perhaps a lump, or a few similar lumps of planetary matter at their centre."

It has also been attempted to apply this theory to the milky way, and the various nebulæ scattered throughout the heavens, by supposing them to be in the transition state, and not yet formed into systems.   The telescope, however, has very satisfactorily proved this to be futile and groundless, as many of these nebulæ are actually resolvable—that is to say, they have been separated by powerful telescopes, and seen to be composed of distinct stars.   Those people who believe that the earth is the only inhabited world in the universe, doubtless believe also that before the creation of Adam there were no inhabitants of any kind even on the earth.   Just entertain this idea for a few moments, while we will endeavour to show how useless and unmeaning must have been the rolling and revolving masses of matter.

Geology tells us of the immensity of the chronology of our world—how long must have been the periods in the formation of the coal strata; how, countless ages back, all our stratified rocks were formed by the gradual deposits at the bottom of the sea; and how they have alternately been heaved up and immersed. Need we inform you, to support us in our statement, how beds of shells and stratified sands have been discovered on the summits of the loftiest mountains, and that the immense beds of chalk, through which our railways cut and tunnel, are composed entirely of fossilized shells?

This fact alone is sufficient to prove how ridiculous is the supposition; nevertheless, we will suppose that throughout these immense periods there were no inhabitants.

" During this long period of universal death, when nature herself was asleep, the sun with his magnificent attendants, the planets with their faithful satellites, the stars in the binary systems, the solar system itself, were performing their daily, their annual, and their secular movements, unseen, unheeded, and fulfilling no purpose that human reason can conceive.

Lamps, lighting nothing; fires, heating nothing; waters, quenching nothing; clouds, screening nothing; breezes, fanning nothing; and every thing around, mountain and valley, hill and dale, earth and ocean, all meaning nothing."*

Unfortunately for those who indulge in such a monstrous notion, the voice of nature speaks in a most convincing manner:—" The investigations of geologists disclose no fact more interesting to mankind than that there are embedded in solid rocks fossil remains of creatures that lived in a former condition of the world, countless ages before man was created.

" These relics reveal to us that during the many revolutions this planet has undergone, different tribes of beings have flourished on the face of the earth, and have become extinct; and that their places have been successively supplied by other forms of animal life, generally of more complicated organization than those which preceded them, and that they have also disappeared. Thus, after many changes, during which the successions of animal and vegetable life more and more nearly approached those of existing genera and species, we arrive at a period when the condition of animated creation

* More Worlds than One, p. 184.

exactly corresponds, in numerous instances, with that of the present."*

With these facts before us, we are induced to believe that, even supposing the other planets are not inhabited by human beings, yet they may have animals of various orders existing on their surfaces, similar to those which existed on our earth prior to the creation of man; but we do not think it exactly right to suppose that all the planets, with the exception of our own, are in this preparatory state—we cannot see any probability of such being the case. We can easily suppose it may be so with some of them, while at the same time it is very probable that others may be in a more advanced state, both morally and physically. But to conceive either one of them—whether it be an enormous mass slumbering in space, or a world like our own, performing its appointed revolutions—to be either altogether void of inhabitants, or not in course of preparation to receive them, is to our mind an idea so monstrously untenable, that we feel amazed and astounded that any one with ordinary understanding should countenance such a doctrine at all, as that of believing in the existence of a universe of void and lifeless matter.

Are we not struck, in studying the works of

* Bakewell's "Illustrated Geology," p. 106.

the Almighty, with the economy displayed in creation—more so, perhaps, than in the manifestation of power? How one purpose is made to subserve others of equal import; how within a nut-shell—to use the phrase—are all the appliances and resources employed in the grandest manifestations of the Omnipotent Creator. This being the case, how can you reconcile this great economy displayed here, while yonder worlds are revolving in unmeaning circles around one great centre? Is it even plausible? Did we believe in separate Deities ruling over each individual sphere, we then could scarcely imagine any of them reigning in lordly magnificence alone. But as we recognise but one Hand and one Ruler, and He that created this world called also the others into existence by the word of His power, we can only imagine that He created one and all for alike beneficent purposes.

Dr. Bentley, in his celebrated argument for the plurality of worlds, says—" That, considering the soul of one virtuous and religious man is of greater worth and excellency than the sun and his planets, and all the stars in the heavens, their usefulness to man might be the sole end of their creation, *if* it could be proved that they were as beneficial to us as the polar star was formerly for navigation, or as the

moon is for producing the tides, and lighting
us on winter nights. But we dare not under-
take to show what advantage is brought to us
by those innumerable stars in the galaxy of other
parts of the firmament, not discernible by naked
eyes, and yet each many thousand times bigger
than the whole body of the earth. If you say they
beget in us a great idea and veneration of the
mighty Author and Governor of such stupendous
bodies, and excite and elevate our minds to His
adoration and praise, you say very truly and
well. But would it not raise in us a higher
apprehension of the infinite majesty and
boundless beneficence of God, to suppose that
those remote and vast bodies were formed, not
merely upon our account, to be peeped at
through an optic glass, but for different ends
and nobler purposes? And yet who will deny
but there are great multitudes of lucid stars
even beyond the reach of the best telescopes;
and that every visible star may have opaque
planets revolving about them, which we cannot
discover? Now, if they were not created for
our sakes, it is certain and evident that they
were not made for their own; for matter
has no life or perception, is not conscious of
its own existence, nor capable of happiness, nor
gives the sacrifice of praise and worship to the
Author of its being, It remains, therefore,

o

that all bodies were formed for the sake of intelligent minds; and as the earth was principally designed for the being and service and contemplation of men, why may not all other planets be created for the like uses, each for their own inhabitants, which have life and understanding?"

Thus far we have been led to consider the subject in its physical and comparative aspect, and have brought to bear upon it the most forcible arguments which analogy and parity of reasoning will warrant us in doing. We now turn to notice the religious consideration of the subject, feeling sure that nothing in our religion or the Bible will be found antagonistic to its principles; or, in other words, we might say, that our belief in the multiplicity of worlds will neither tend to falsify or invalidate one single truth set forth in Holy Writ. In fact, we have not to look very far into those pages without finding great support to this doctrine. Perhaps the first text which occurs is in the 2nd chapter of Genesis, and the 1st verse :—— " Thus the heavens and the earth were finished, and all the host of them." Now, at first sight, perhaps, the last clause of this verse may be taken to mean the stars themselves; but this cannot be, as they from necessity must be included in what goes before—" the heavens." What, then, is the meaning of the expression? "All the host *of* them" can only mean the inhabitants of the heavens and the earth. That little word "*of*" speaks volumes; it signifies possession, and the verse might very well read—"Thus the heavens and the earth were finished, and all the host *they possess.*" In Psalm xxxiii. 6, we read—"By the word of the Lord were the heavens made; and all the host of them by the breath of His mouth." This, it will be observed, is still more forcible; it refers distinctly and separately—first, to the creation of the heavens by His command; and, secondly, how the host of the inhabitants received their being. Precisely similar, you will remark, to the way in which Adam received his life: "And the Lord God formed man of the dust of the ground, and breathed into his nostrils the breath of life; and man became a living soul." *

In Nehemiah ix. 6, we read—"Thou hast made heaven, the heaven of heavens, with all their host, the earth, and all things that are therein, the seas, and all that therein is, and thou preservest them all; and the host of heaven worshippeth thee."

Here we have the host of heaven referred to as worshipping God. Now, we cannot suppose

* Genesis ii. 7.

for a moment that the "host" here spoken of can mean enormous lumps of chaotic matter. Where is its power for worship?

> "Has matter more than motion?   Has it thought,
>   Judgment, and genius?"

No; and therefore the text must refer to beings possessing intellectual capacities, like unto ourselves.   And then again, in various parts of the Old and New Testament, we find the heavens referred to as a separate and distinct creation from the world; and there are numerous passages which very clearly indicate that they are the seat of life.   In the 45th chapter of Isaiah, and the 12th verse, we read—" I have made the earth, and created man upon it : I, even my hands, have stretched out the heavens, and all their host have I commanded."

Here you have them both separately referred to—the earth and its inhabitants, man; and the host who inhabit the heavens, being commanded by God.

In the 18th verse of the same chapter we read, "For thus saith the Lord that created the heavens; God himself that formed the earth and made it; He hath established it, He created it not in vain; He formed it to be inhabited."   In this we have it inferred, that

had the earth not been intended to be inhabited; it would have been created in vain.
Surely, then, if all those shining orbs, and all
those revolving planets, are not inhabited, they
must have been created in vain. But we must
not dare to say so; He created them also,
" not in vain," but doubtless formed them " to
be inhabited." Isaiah also speaks of the
heavens being " spread out as a tent to dwell
in."

Many other quotations of a like and equally
forcible nature might be brought forward to
substantiate our belief in the multiplicity of
worlds, but we take it that those we have
already quoted will be found sufficiently forcible
to assure those who may have had doubts on
the subject, that biblical support is not wanting
to enhance our belief.

Many attempts have been made by the wicked
and designing to persuade people that the
results and discoveries of science have proved
to be antagonistic to some of the most che-
rished doctrines of religion and Scripture. In
former times this was carried to such an excess
that many have forfeited their lives as a sacrifice for the scientific truths which they enter-
tained. Take, for instance, the old controversy
as to whether the earth revolved round the
sun, or the sun round the earth; and inte-

resting, indeed, are the respective histories of
Copernicus and Galileo. On one occasion,
Galileo, in writing to Kepler, said, " Oh, my
dear Kepler, how I wish that we could have
one hearty laugh together.   Here, at Padua, is
the Principal Professor of Philosophy, whom I
have repeatedly and urgently requested to look
at the moon and planets through my glass,
which he pertinaciously refuses to do.   Why
are you not here ?   What shouts of laughter
we should have at this glorious folly, and to
hèar the Professor of Philosophy at Pisa
labouring before the Grand Duke with logical
arguments, as if with magical incantations, to
charm the new planets out of the sky."   But a
fearful cloud was now rising over Galileo, which
spread itself, and grew darker every hour.   The
Church of Rome had taken alarm at the new
doctrines respecting the earth's motion, as
contrary to the declarations of the Bible, and
a formidable difficulty presented itself; namely,
how to publish and defend these doctrines,
without invoking the terrible punishments in-
flicted by the Inquisition on heretics.   No
work could be printed without license from the
Court of Rome; and any opinions supposed to
be held, and much more known to be taught by
any one, which by an ignorant and supersti-
tious priesthood could be intrepreted as con-

trary to Scripture, would expose the offender to the severest punishment, even to imprisonment, scourging, and death. We, who live in an age so distinguished for freedom of thought and opinion, can form but a very inadequate conception of the bondage in which the minds of men were held by the chains of the Inquisition. It was necessary, therefore, for Galileo to proceed with the greatest caution in promulgating truths which his own discoveries had confirmed. He did not, like the Christian martyrs, proclaim the truth in the face of persecutions and tortures; but while he sought to give currency to the Copernican doctrines, he laboured at the same time, by cunning artifices, to blind the ecclesiastics to his real designs, and thus to escape the effects of their hostility.

Before Galileo published his doctrines in form, he had expressed himself so freely as to have excited much alarm among the ecclesiastics. One of them preached publicly against him, taking for his text the passage, " Ye men of Galilee, why stand ye here gazing up into heaven?" He therefore thought it prudent to resort to Rome, and confront his enemies face to face.

A contemporary describes his appearance there in the following terms, in a letter addressed to a Romish cardinal:—" Your Eminence would be delighted with Galileo, if you heard him holding forth, as he often does, in the midst of fifteen or twenty, all violently attacking him, sometimes in one house, sometimes in another. But he is armed after such fashion that he laughs all of them to scorn; and even if the novelty of his opinions prevents entire persuasion, at least he convicts of emptiness most of the arguments with which his adversaries endeavour to overwhelm him."

In 1616, Galileo, as he himself states, had a most gracious audience of the Pope, Paul V., which lasted for nearly an hour; at the end of which his Holiness assured him, that the Convocation were no longer in a humour to listen lightly to calumnies against him, and that so long as he occupied the Papal chair, Galileo might think himself out of all danger. Nevertheless, he was not allowed to return home without receiving formal notice not to teach the opinions of Copernicus, " that the sun is in the centre of the system, and that the earth moves about it," from that time forward in any manner.*

From this time forth he was subject to many persecutions, and eventually, " At the age of seventy," says Dr. Brewster, in his life of Sir

* The Orbs of Heaven.

Isaac Newton, " on his bended knees, and with his right hand resting on the Holy Evangelists, did this patriarch of science avow his present and past belief in the dogmas of the Romish Church, abandon as false and heretical the doctrine of the earth's motion and of the sun's immobility, and pledge himself to denounce to the Inquisition any other person who was even suspected of heresy. He abjured, cursed, and detested those eternal and immutable truths which the Almighty had permitted him to be the first to establish. Had Galileo but added the courage of a martyr to the wisdom of the sage; had he carried the glance of his indignant eye round the circle of his judges; had he lifted his hands to heaven, and called upon the living God to witness the truth and immutability of his opinions, the bigotry of his enemies would have been disarmed, and science would have enjoyed a memorable triumph."

We have entered at some length into the troubles which beset Galileo, as they show forth the difficulties under which scientific truth laboured in the past ages. But we, at least, have the satisfaction of seeing all these controversies terminating in favour of science; and no matter whether it be astronomy or whether it be geology, or whether it be any other division of science, we rejoice in the fact that they all, ultimately, not only are found in accordance with Scripture, but often explain truths which, but for them, would remain inexplicable mysteries.

It has been asked, if it is likely, supposing such an infinity of worlds to be inhabited, that God would send His Son to suffer and die for the inhabitants of such an insignificant portion of His universe as this earth occupies? But those who argue in this way must surely forget the omniscience and omnipotency of the Creator, must forget that a sparrow does not fall to the ground without His notice, and that even the hairs of our head are numbered. And then, again, we know not how the death of our Saviour may affect the inhabitants of other worlds; for since the inhabitants of the earth have sinned, and require a Saviour, the inhabitants of other worlds may have sinned, and require a Saviour also. If we suppose otherwise, and imagine that those worlds are peopled by beings who have kept their first estate, we may as well give up the idea of their being inhabited at all, since analogy fails us. We cannot imagine that beings who are like ourselves subject to the laws of the material universe, are free from sin and imperfections, and the consequences arising therefrom.

" Men of lofty minds and of undoubted piety

have regarded the existence of moral evil as a necessary part of the general scheme of the universe, and consequently as affecting all its rational inhabitants; the race of Adam on our own globe, and the races, perchance, more glorious than ours in the planets around us, and in the remotest system in space.

" When on the eve of learning the truth of his opinions, the illustrious Huygens did not hesitate to affirm that it would be absurd to suppose that all things were made otherwise than God willed, and knew, would happen; and that if we had lived in continual peace, and with an abundant supply of all the good things of this life, there would have been neither art nor science, and the human race would soon have lived like the brutes that perish. And with these views he comes to the conclusion, that the inhabitants of the other planets must be endowed with the same vices and virtues as man, because without such vices and virtues they would be far more degraded than the occupants of the earth." *

Mr. Hugh Miller, a man of profound thought, writes, in a book entitled " Footprints of the Creator," as follows :—

" From the revealed record we learn that the dynasty of man in the mixed state and

* More Worlds than One, p. 143.

character is not the final one, but that there is
to be yet another creation, or more properly
re-creation, known theologically as the resurrection, which shall be connected in its physical
components by bonds of mysterious paternity
with the dynasty which now reigns, and be
bound to it mentally by the chain of identity,
conscious and actual; but which, in all that
constitutes superiority, shall be as vastly its
superior as the dynasty of responsible man is
superior to even the lowest of the preliminary
dynasties.   We are further taught that, at the
commencement of this last of the dynasties, there
will be a re-creation of not only elevated, but also
of degraded beings—a re-creation of the lost.
We are taught yet further, that though the
present dynasty be that of a lapsed race, which
at their first introduction were placed on
higher ground than that on which they now
stand, and sank by their own act; it was yet
part of the original design, from the beginning
of all things, that they should occupy the
existing platform; and that redemption is thus
no after-thought, rendered necessary by the
fall; but, on the contrary, part of a general
scheme, for which provision has been made
from the beginning; so that the Divine Man,
through whom the work of restoration has
been effected, was in reality, in reference to

the purposes of the Eternal, what He is
designated in the remarkable text, ' the Lamb
slain from the foundation of the world!'
Slain from the foundation of the world!
Could the assertors of the stony science ask
for language more express? By piecing the
two records together—that revealed in Scripture, and that revealed in rocks—records
which, however widely geologists may mistake the one, or commentators misunderstand
the other, have emanated from the same great
Author, we learn that in slow and solemn
majesty has period succeeded period, each in
succession ushering in a higher and yet higher
scene of existence—that fish, reptiles, mam-
miferous quadrupeds, have reigned in turn;
that responsible man, ' made in the image of
God,' and with dominion over all creatures,
ultimately entered into a world ripened for his
reception; but further, that this passing scene,
in which he forms the prominent figure, is not
the final one in the long series, but merely the
last of the *preliminary* scenes; and that that
period to which the bygone ages, incalculable
in amount, with all their well-proportioned
gradations of being, form the imposing vestibule, shall have perfection for its occupant,
and eternity for its duration. I know not
how it may appear to others, but for my own

part I cannot avoid thinking that there would be a lack of proportion in the series of being, were the period of perfect and glorified humanity abruptly connected, *without the introduction of an intermediate creation of responsible imperfection*, with that of the dying irresponsible brute. That scene of things in which God became man and suffered, *seems*, as it no doubt *is*, a necessary link in the chain."

> " All nature is but art, unknown to thee;
>   All chance, direction which thou canst not see;
>   All discord, harmony not understood;
>   All partial evil, universal good."—POPE.

This brings us to the inquiry, as to where man, in his future state of existence, is likely to reside ? He will then have, as now, a spiritual nature and a corporeal frame, and therefore must live in a material world. Now, at the present time there are existing on the earth upwards of a thousand millions of inhabitants; and if to these you add those who have gone before, and those who may follow after, it will be clearly evident that the earth will not be able to accommodate them all. Where, then, we ask, after the resurrection, are they to go, if not to some planet whose inhabitants have ceased to exist, or to planets, either in our own or other systems, which have been in a state of preparation for the reception of intellectual life? For our part, we believe that every portion of the universe may be visited at will by the redeemed, and be successively their abode; and that they may be permitted to fly with the speed of lightning from one world to another, and contemplate the wonders of the Almighty, which may be so differently displayed.

Respecting the future of the universe, we know nothing very definite; we can only surmise, and draw inferences from various parts of Scripture. But do not ask us to interpret revelation as literal; it is figurative, certainly for the most part, if not the whole; all things will be new to us, because they will be changed, but in no other sense can this be interpreted. The world is to be destroyed by fire, we read; but we take this as referring to the wicked who may remain in sin and unbelief at the last great day, and who will perish in the flames, as did the inhabitants of the earth in the time of Noah by water. Scripture, however, does not tell us where the abode of the blessed will be, or what part of the universe they may inhabit; it does not state where the house of many mansions is situate, or in what region of space these mansions are built; but it is impossible almost to doubt, that some of those celestial spheres are to be our future homes.

With this we conclude, feeling assured that whether it be the student of astronomy, or the truth-seeking philosopher, or the loving and faithful Christian, neither will regard the starry firmament with less interest, for contemplating so interesting an inquiry as to the great probability of a *multiplicity of worlds*.

" Say why was man so eminently raised,
  Amid the vast creation; why ordained
  Through life and death to dart his piercing eye,
  With thoughts beyond the limits of his frame ;
  But that the Omnipotent might send him forth
  In sight of mortal and immortal powers,
  As on a boundless theatre, to run
  The great career of justice; to exalt
  His generous aim to all diviner deeds ;
  To chase each partial purpose from his breast;
  And through the mists of passion and of sense,
  And through the tossing tide of chance and pain,
  To hold his course unfaltering, while the voice
  Of truth and virtue up the steep ascent
  Of nature calls him to his high reward,
  The applauding smile of Heaven? Else wherefore
    burns
  In mortal bosoms this unquenched hope,
  That breathes from day to day sublimer things,
  And mocks possession ? Wherefore darts the mind
  With such resistless ardour to embrace
  Majestic forms; impatient to be free,
  Spurning the gross control of wilful might:
  Proud of the strong contention of her toils—
  Proud to be daring?   Who but rather turns
  To heaven's broad fire his unconstrained view,
  Than to the glimmering of a waxen flame ?

Who that from Alpine heights his labouring eye
Shoots round the wide horizon, to survey
Nilus or Ganges rolling his bright wave
Through mountains, plains, through empires black
   with shade,
And continents of sand, will turn his gaze
To mark the windings of a scanty rill
That murmurs at his feet? The high-born soul
Disdains to rest her heaven-aspiring wing
Beneath its native quarry.   Tired of earth
And this diurnal scene, she springs aloft
Through fields of air; pursues the flying storm;
Rides on the volley'd lightning through the heavens;
Or, yoked with whirlwinds and the northern blast,
Sweeps the long track of day.   Then high she soars
The blue profound, and, hovering round the sun,
Beholds him pouring the redundant stream
Of light; beholds his unrelenting sway
Bend the reluctant planets to absolve
The fated rounds of time.   Thence far effused
She darts her swiftness up the long career
Of devious comets; through its burning signs
Exulting measures the perennial wheel
Of nature, and looks back on all the stars,
Those blended lights, as with a milky zone,
Invest the orient.   Now amazed she views
The empyreal waste, where happy spirits hold,
Beyond this concave heaven, their calm abode;
And fields of radiance, whose unfading light
Has travelled the profound six thousand years,
Nor yet arrived in sight of mortal things.
Even on the barriers of the world, untired,
She meditates the eternal depth below;
Till, half recoiling, down the headlong steep
She plunges—soon o'erwhelmed and swallowed up
In that immense of being.   There her hopes

P

Rest at the fated goal.   For from the birth
Of mortal man, the sovereign Maker said,
That not in humble nor in brief delight,
Not in the fading echoes of renown;
Power's purple robes, nor pleasure's flowery lap,
The soul should find enjoyment; but from these
Turning disdainful to an equal good,
Through all the ascent of things enlarge her view,
Till every bound at length should disappear,
And infinite perfection close the scene."

AKENSIDE.

GEORGE UNWIN, GRESHAM STEAM PRESS, BUCKLERSBURY.

THE JAPANESE;
THEIR MANNERS AND CUSTOMS.

BY

THOMAS CLARK WESTFIELD.

Illustrated with Photographic Views, and Portraits of the Japanese Commissioners, taken in Japan,

BY MESSRS. NEGRETTI AND ZAMBRA.

LIST OF ILLUSTRATIONS.

1. Portraits of the Japanese Ambassadors.
2. Port of Kanagawa, with Shipping.
3. Town and Bay of Kanagawa.
4. The Emperor's Temple at Jedda.
5. Cemetery of the Nobles and Princes at Jedda.
6. Portraits of Japanese Ladies in Full Dress.

OPINIONS OF THE PRESS.

ENGLISH NEWS, 5 *Aug.*, 1862.—"The Japanese; their Manners and Customs," is the title of an exquisite work by Thomas Clark Westfield, Esq. It is in quarto form, beautifully printed, and, taking the Photographs and the text together, an unexpected insight is afforded into Japanese life, Japanese ideas, and Japanese customs. As there is no other book of the kind, it is a necessary acquisition to every library, and should adorn the table of every drawing-room.

LONDON REVIEW, 8 *Feb.*, 1862.—The value of this little work consists in the Photographic Views which it contains. They are beautifully executed, and the letter-press is just sufficiently long to explain the subjects.

PHOTOGRAPHIC NEWS, 14 *Feb.*, 1862.—The substance of this work was originally delivered as a Lecture at the Marylebone Literary and Scientific Institution. It contains a careful *resumé* of the best information which various explorers have contributed respecting a country and people. The work is very handsomely got up in small quarto. It is well printed, and handsomely bound; and the Photographs are on tinted mounts, with ample margin. Altogether the volume will adorn worthily the drawing-room table.

LONDON: THOMAS PIPER, 32, PATERNOSTER ROW.

Lightning Source UK Ltd.
Milton Keynes UK
UKHW031840100821
388610UK00008B/1678